The Association
of Illustrators present

images
17

acknowledgments

The AOI would like to thank:

all Images 17 judges: Sophie Ross, Susan Christie, Carolyn Luton, Ruth Gladwin, Simon Farr, Pauline Hazelwood, Michael Bramman, Gale Pitt, Guitty Talberg, Margaret Welbank, Annabel Wilson, George Caldwell, Chris Mackenzie, Fionna Purcell, Still Price Lintas advertising agency and anyone else who helped make this project a reality.

Thanks to Eva for an extraordinary effort, Ron for pulling strings, Claire for uncommon faith and Nick and Alan for staying cool and blinding design.

David O'Sullivan
Publisher

ISBN 0 9520326 0 0

Publisher
David O'Sullivan
Trojan Horse Publishing

Editor and Competition Organiser
Claire Mackenzie

Design and Typesetting
The Binding Brown Partnership

Cover Painting
Nick Brown

Sales
Eva Zwill

Warehousing and Distribution
Ron Philpott

Colour Reproduction
Trinity Graphic Company,
Hong Kong

Printing
Industown Printing Associates,
Hong Kong

Now in its seventeenth year, the Images Annual and exhibition remains the major event showcasing British illustration at its best. The seven sections in which the competition is judged represent the main areas in which illustration is commissioned and comprises the Winners section.

This Annual shows the majority of the work selected by the seven eminent judging panels for inclusion in Images 17.

This years exhibition began with a Grand Launch at the premises of Still Price Lintas advertising agency, where the work was displayed and shown to many commissioning clients.

This year the book has also changed in format. Two extra sections are included: the Professionals' section and the Newcomers' section. Both showcase illustration worthy of note which has been selected for its quality.

We hope you take pleasure from viewing this fine collection of the best of British illustration. We think it shows why British illustration is world renowned for creativity and talent.

The Association of Illustrators was established in 1973 in order to advance and protect illustrators rights, encourage professional standards and the use of illustration in the communications industry. The AOI is a non-profit making trade association dedicated to its members; to protect their interests and promote their work.

The membership of about 1,500 consists primarily of freelance illustrators as well as agents, clients, students and tutors. The AOI retains two full-time employees and a part-time financial manager and it is run by ten council members elected at the AGM.

The AOI is the only body to represent and campaign for illustrators rights. It has improved the standing of illustration as a profession and increased recognition among clients of the power of illustration to communicate.

1992 has been a year of change for the AOI. This is the first year they have produced the annual without sponsorship from a publisher. This could not have been possible without the unswerving positivity of our publisher, Trojan Horse Publishing. We have also moved premises into Bedford Square with the Chartered Society of Designers, the Industry lead body for design and the Design Business Association. This reinforces the Association's aim of working within the creative industry alongside sister organisations.

intro

contents

winners

information and technical

Professional and student information and technical illustration includes architectural drawings, natural history and medical illustration for any use.

Judges

David Gifford	Illustrator
Bob Hook	Readers' Digest
Michael Leek	Bournemouth & Poole College
Jonathan Potter	Illustrator
Giles Velarde	Exhibition Consultant

simon williams

c/o Bournemouth & Poole College
of Art & Design
Wallisdown Road
Poole
Dorset
BH12 5HH

t: 0202 533011

Title
The Four Masted Barque 'Pommern', 1903

Medium
Watercolour and gouache

Purpose of work
Museum display and poster illustration

Brief
To produce a full colour measured perspective illustration of the ship as she was during her career under the Gustaf Erikson house flag, 1923-1947, Mariehamn, Aland, Finland.

Commissioned by
Jyrki Abrahamsson,
Musiefartyget Pommern

malcolm tween

c/o Bournemouth & Poole College of
Art & Design
Wallisdown Road
Poole
Dorset
BH12 5HH

t: 0202 533011

Title
Recovery Vehicle Wheeled
(General Service) 6 x 6 Foden

Medium
Watercolour and gouache airbrush

Purpose of work
Museum Poster

Brief
To produce a full colour measured perspective illustration of the vehicle showing all salient features, but with sufficient interest and appeal for a wider audience in particular visitors to the proposed museum.

Commissioned by
Lt. Col. Larry Le Var REME (Retd),
The Trustees of the Royal Electrical and Mechanical Engineers Museum

lee pascoe

Falmouth School of Art & Design
Design & Illustration Annexe
Trevenson Road
Pool
Redruth
Cornwall
TR15 3PJ
t: 0209 612004

Title
The Great Barrier Reef

Medium
Gouache and ink

Purpose of work
College

Brief
To illustrate a reef with a selection of its natural inhabitants.

c/o Bournemouth &
Poole College of Art &
Design
Wallisdown Road
Poole
Dorset
BH12 5HH

t: 0202 533011

Title
Seagull 50cc Out-board
Marine Engine

Medium
Ink, line and gouache
airbrush

Purpose of work
College project

Brief
To provide a measured
cutaway perspective
illustration working
from the full-size
engine and showing all
salient features with
the propeller and its
immediate shafting
arrangement rendered
in full colour.

Commissioned by
College,
Sabre Engines Limited

dean chapman

63 Aldbourne Road
Shepherds Bush
London
W12

t: 081 749 5490

Title
Firefighting Equipment

Medium
Ink and watercolour

Purpose of work
Informational poster

Brief
To show the range of equipment carried by a modern fire engine.

Firefighting equipment

winners

print and design

Work commissioned for use in packaging, record sleeves, calendars, stationery, annual reports, brochures, catalogues, greeting cards for commercial or private use (if commissioned by someone other than the artist).

Judges

Ray Ally	Fitch RS
Flo Bayley	Paperchase
Margaret Chapman	Chambers Chapman
Andres Hunter	McIlroy Coates
Kathyrn Tattershall	Tattershall Hammarling Silk

david sim

5 Cobden Crescent
Edinburgh
EH9 2BG

t: 031 667 8592

Title
Christmas Table

Medium
Watercolour, coloured paper, ink, collage

Purpose of work
Christmas card

Brief
Produce an image of Christmas food and table setting for use as a Christmas card for catering company.

Commissioned by
Jessica Smith,
Allied and Catering

fletcher sibthorp

134 Salcott Road
London
SW11 6DG

t: 071 924 2473

Title
Rhythmic Gymnast

Medium
Mixed media on canvas

Purpose of work
For cards and limited edition prints

Brief
To produce a painting conveying the power and dexterity of gymnasts.

Commissioned by
P Arnott,
The Stable Gallery

zafer baran

7 Denbigh Gardens
Richmond
TW10 6EN

t: 081 948 3050

Title
Tree Suicide

Medium
Mixed

Purpose of work
To illustrate WWF Annual Review

Brief
A free brief, covering WWF's areas of interest, and particularly environmental degradation and the need for a more caring approach.

Commissioned by
John Scully and John Dunne, Dunne & Scully

Client
World Wide Fund for Nature (WWF), Geneva

7 Denbigh Gardens
Richmond
TW10 6EN

t: 081 948 3050

Title
Interdependence

Medium
Mixed

Purpose of work
To illustrate WWF Annual Review

Brief
A free brief, covering WWF's areas of interest, and particularly environmental degradation and the need for a more caring approach.

Commissioned by
John Scully and John Dunne, Dunne & Scully

Client
World Wide Fund for Nature (WWF), Geneva

zafer baran

7 Denbigh Gardens
Richmond
TW10 6EN

t: 081 948 3050

Title
Message In A Bottle

Medium
Mixed

Purpose of work
To illustrate WWF Annual Review

Brief
A free brief, covering WWF's areas of interest, and particularly environmental degradation and the need for a more caring approach.

Commissioned by
John Scully and John Dunne, Dunne & Scully

Client
World Wide Fund for Nature (WWF), Geneva

vikki liogier

13 Kay Road
London
SW9 9DF
t: 071 274 3789
f: 071 274 3789

Title
After The Performance, The Reward

Medium
Line and collage

Purpose of work
Cover illustration for brochure

Brief
To produce an illustration emphasising the reward from tax-free gains from investments.

Commissioned by
Judy Dalgleish, Touche Remnant Unit Trust Management Limited

robert heesom

6 Cyril Mansions
Prince of Wales Drive
London
SW11 4HR

t: 071 498 0684

Title
USA Finance

Medium
Acrylic

Purpose of Work
Brochure Illustration

Brief
Show how the County Natwest Investment Management Team can help investors in the USA financial markets.

Commissioned by
Neil Littman, Pauffley & Company

Client
County Natwest Investment Management Limited

33 Eswyn Road
Tooting
London
SW17 8TR

t: 081 767 2618

Title
Shipping Composition

Medium
Acrylic

Purpose of work
Cover for annual report and accounts

Brief
Open brief to include elements of the companiy's business (ie shipping insurers).

Commissioned by
David Pearce,
Tatham Pearce

Client
Assurance Foreningen Gard

MAGNET
ARTISTS

sarah ball

43 Kemsing Road
Greenwich
London
SE10 0LL

t: 071 613 2620

Title
The Recruiting Officer

Medium
Chalk Pastel

Purpose of work
Theatre Poster

Brief
To read the script and create an image to describe the feelings, the time and the events of the play.

Commissioned by
Michael Mayhew, The Royal National Theatre

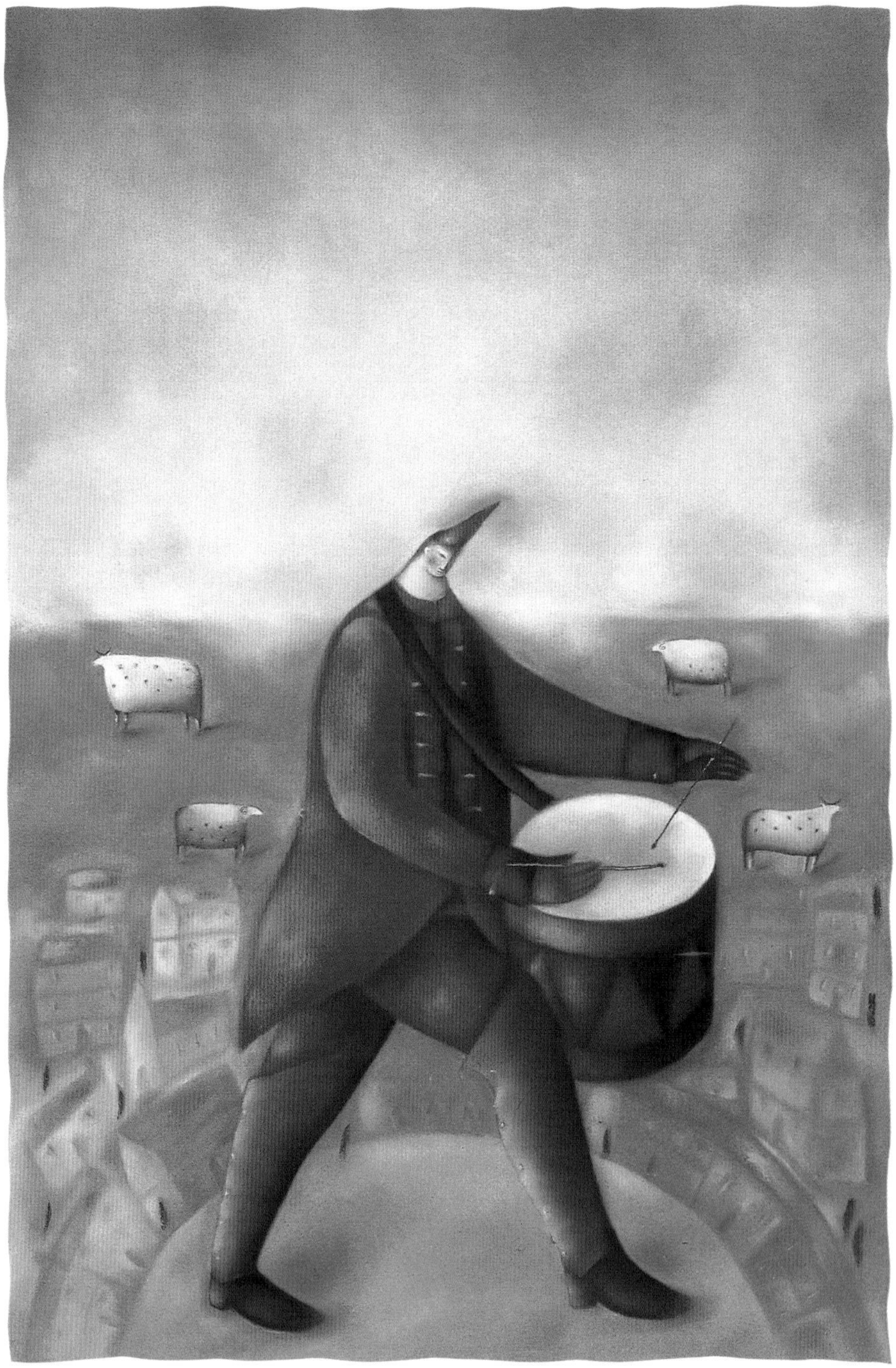

nancy anderson

8A Birdhurst Rise
South Croydon
Surrey
CR2 7ED

t: 081 681 0310

Title
Natural Power

Medium
Linocut and watercolour

Purpose of work
Brochure for National Engineering Laboratory Power Systems

Brief
The laboratory carries out research and tests natural power systems. They wanted a strip to be used on the brochure cover which could also be separated and used inside with text.

Commissioned by
Dorothy Clarkson-Smith, Department of Trade and Industry

michael sheehy

115 Crystal Palace Rd
East Dulwich
London
SE22 9ES

t: 081 693 4315

Title
Large Companies Leave Small Companies Out In The Cold

Medium
Mixed Media

Purpose of work
Brochure about 'Business in the New Europe'

Brief
Large companies are likely to become more powerful within a European Business Community. They will utilize the services of medium-sized companies, but small companies are likely to lose out entirely.

Commissioned by
Mike Lackersteen, Esterson Lackersteen

Client
Andersen Consulting

99 Tregenna Avenue
South Harrow
Middlesex
HA2 8QP

t: 081 423 6486

Title
A Modern Icarus Films
The Sun

Medium
Acrylic

Purpose of work
Brochure cover

Brief
To produce an image reflecting the production facilities at Yorkshire Television, the image had to be very striking with an original and distinctive style and idea.

Commissioned by
Geoff Collins,
Yorkshire Television

winners

editorial

Work commissioned for editorial purposes in newspapers and magazines

Judges

Julian Barrett	Bella
David Eachus	Director Magazine
Chris Krage	Saturday Times Review
Anne Morrow	The Guardian
Sharon Wooten	Marketing Business Magazine

7 Queensgate Villas
Victoria Park Road
London
E9 7BU

t: 071 986 2441

Title
Cogito Ergo Sum

Medium
Pen ink and watercolour

Purpose of work
To accompany magazine article

Brief
To illustrate an article about artificial intelligence.

Commissioned by
Colin Brewster,
New Scientist (IPC)

paul slater

22 Partridge Close
Chesham
HP5 3LH

t: 0494 786780

Title
Pizza (After Norman Rockwell)

Medium
Acrylic

Purpose of work
To illustrate restaurant review in magazine

Brief
Standardization of the pizza through pizza chains.

Commissioned by
Chris Krage,
The Times
Saturday Review

Fernleigh
Huntingdon Road
Houghton
Huntingdon
Cambridgeshire
PE17 2AU

t: 0480 61506

Title
All Genomes Great and Small

Medium
Scraperboard, acrylic and ink

Purpose of work
To accompany a report on a Genome Conference

Brief
To show some of the hundreds of strands of research involved in the 'Human Genome Project', an international effort to decode all genetic information in human chromosomes.

Commissioned by
Pip Nielsen, New Scientist

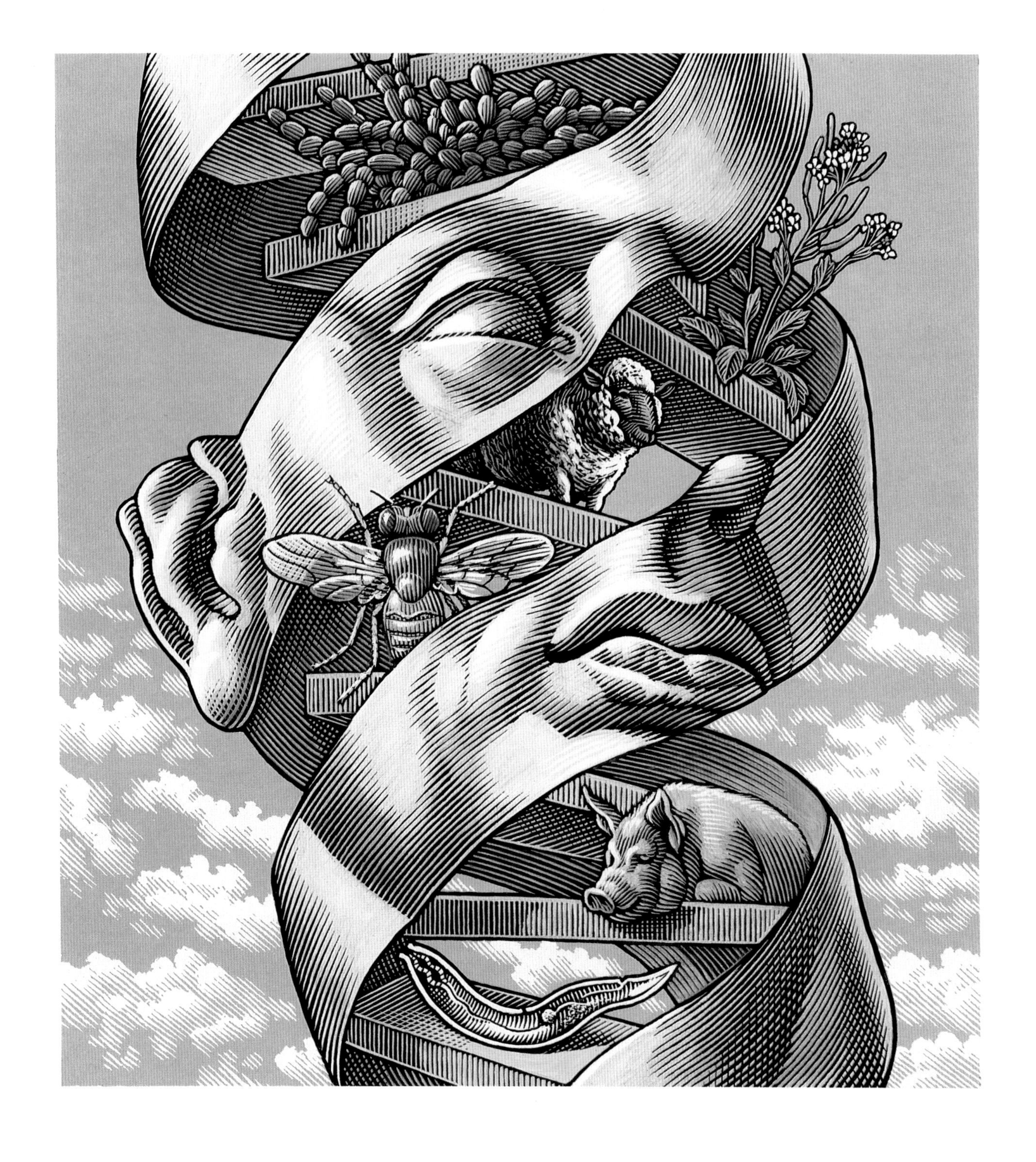

liz sanders

Consumers' Association
2 Marylebone Road
London
NW1 4DE

t: 071 486 5544

Title
Breakfast Time

Medium
Breakfast cereals and glue on board

Purpose of work
Front cover image for Which? magazine

Brief
To construct an image reminiscent of a breakfast cereal packet (but not resembling any particular packaging).

Illustration to be entirely assembled using wide range of cereals.

Commissioned by
Ian Price,
Which?, Consumers' Association

eric robson

72 North Avenue
Southend-on-Sea
Essex
SS2 5HU

t: 0702 469936

Agent
Garden Studio

t: 071 287 9191

Title
Rainforest Monkeys and Apes

Medium
Watercolour

Purpose of work
Centre-spread of a magazine

Brief
A list of twenty species of monkeys and apes to be incorporated in an appropriate rain-forest habitat.

Commissioned by
Alan Ashby

Client
'Wild About Animals'

ian murray

10 Essex Avenue
Didsbury
Manchester
M20 0AN

t: 061 448 0260

Title
"Astroman"

Medium
Gouache, ink,
varnish, collage

Purpose
Editorial

Brief
To represent the way in which business uses astrology in the selection of new employees.

Commissioned by
Chris Krage,
Times Saturday Review

ian murray

10 Essex Avenue
Didsbury
Manchester
M20 0AN

t: 061 448 0260

Title
In The Cannes

Medium
Gouache, ink
and varnish

Purpose of work
Cover of magazine

Brief
To represent a hotel in the South of France which hosts a 'party' for TV producers etc..

Commissioned by
Fiona Matthias, TV Producer Magazine

helen jones

1A Elia Street
London
N1 8DE

t: 071 837 1160
071 837 0509

Title
Physics Comes Back Down to Earth

Medium
Mixed

Purpose of work
Spot illustration to accompany magazine article

Brief
The general perception of physics is of big-bang theory astronomy, of making big discoveries; but physics can also be about abstract thought, an end in itself not a means to an end.

Commissioned by
Steve De Vane/ David Eachus, Director Publications

robert heesom

6 Cyril Mansions
Prince of Wales Drive
London
SW11 4HR

t: 071 498 0684

Title
Science and Spirit

Medium
Acrylic

Purpose of Work
Illustrating article

Brief
In an age dominated by science and technology is there still a relevance in spiritual and religious thought on the origins of the Universe.

Commissioned by
David Curless,
Times Saturday Review

christopher gunson

63 Sudbury Court
Allen Edwards Drive
London
SW8 2NT

t: 071 622 7559

Title
Psychiatric Intensive Care

Medium
Ink

Purpose of work
To illustrate magazine article

Brief
The role of the psychiatric intensive care unit

Commissioned By
Lizz Terrell,
Nursing Times, Macmillan Magazines

geoff grandfield

75 Church Walk
London
N16 8QR

t: 071 241 1523

Title
Reclaiming the True Faith for Women

Medium
Chalk pastel

Purpose of work
Editorial

Brief
The article by Rana Kabbani

Commissioned by
The Guardian

carolyn gowdy

2C Maynard Close
Off Cambria Street
London
SW6 2EN

t: 071 731 5380

Title
Truth Or Dare

Medium
Mixed

Purpose of work
To illustrate a weekly column by Clement Freud

Brief
About learning the difference between right and wrong.

Commissioned by
Chris Krage,
Times Saturday Review

claire fletcher

Redwood Publishing
101 Bayham Street
London
NW1

t: 071 331 8000

Title
Not a Thing to Wear

Medium
Acrylic Paints

Purpose of work
Illustration for article

Brief
'The art of packing' · produce illustration fitting that article.

Commissioned by
Lisa Clarke,
Redwood, Clothes Show Magazine Publishing

max ellis

22 Thorney Hedge Rd
Chiswick
London
W4 5SD

t: 081 995 4771

Title
Beelzebob

Medium
Acrylic

Purpose of work
Illustrating magazine article

Brief
Depict the late Maxwell in aggressive painted portraiture.

Commissioned by
Paul Bowden / Alison Pincott,
British GQ, Conde Nast

chris burke

76 Auckland Road
Tunbridge Wells
Kent
TN1 2HS

t: 0892 531329

Title
Not The Valentine Show

Medium
Mixed

Purpose of work
Radio page illustration to launch new TV/Radio section of Sunday Times

Brief
Illustration for 'Not the Valentine Show' Radio II 14th February. The antidote to St Valentines Day, songs include D.I.V.O.R.C.E., You're Moving Out Today, Thorn In My Side, etc..

Commissioned by
Lucy Pidduck, Sunday Times

paul burgess

73 Pascoe Road
Hither Green
London
SE13 5JE

t: 081 852 1600
f: 081 852 1600

Title
Chattanooga Choo Choo

Medium
Collage/Mixed Media

Purpose of work
Part 1 of a 6 part series, 'Across America by Songtitle'

Brief
Illustrate an article on Chattanooga, related to famous Glenn Miller song, also showing historical, social and cultural elements.

Commissioned by
Raymonde Watkins,
Telegraph Magazine

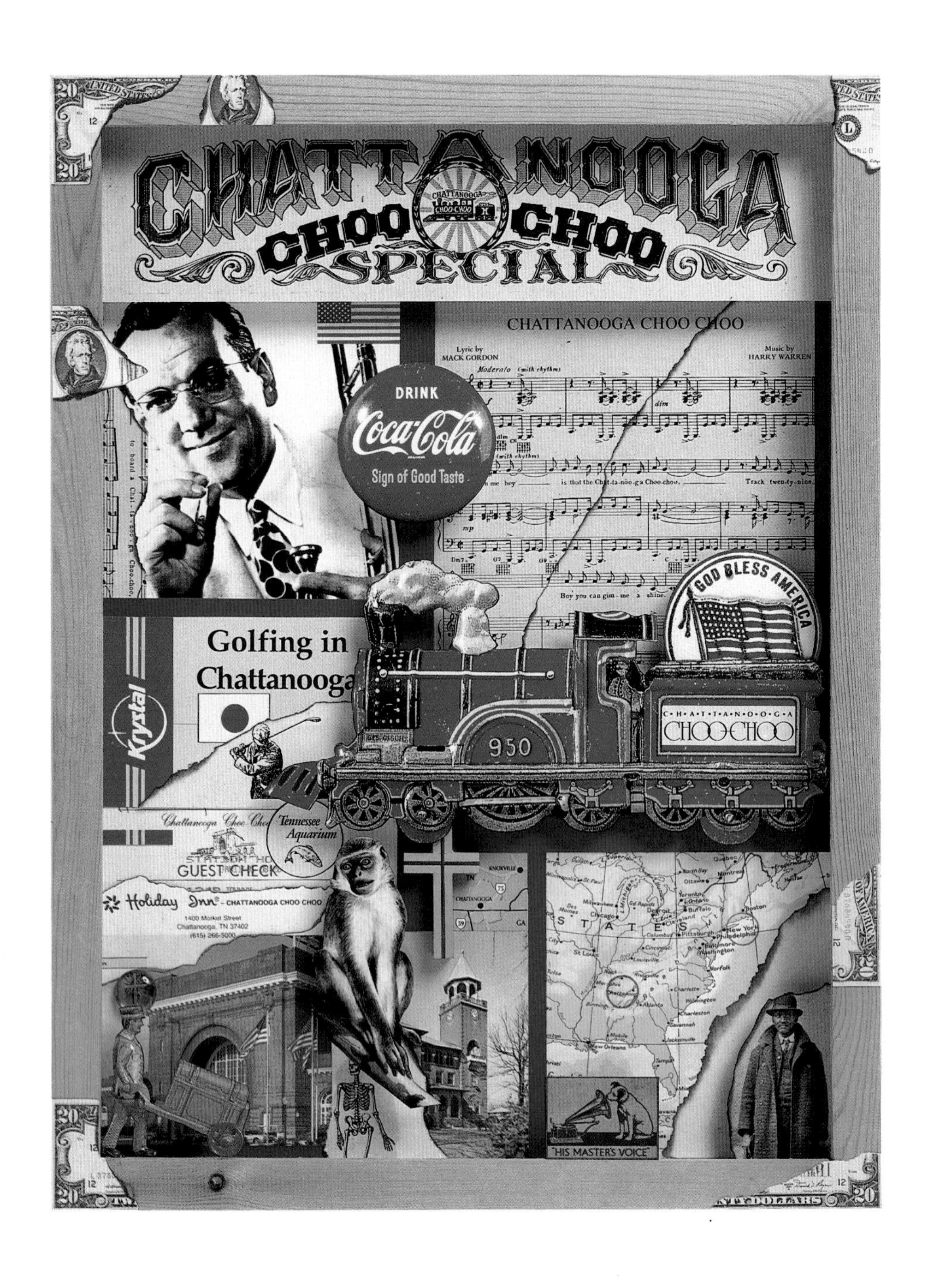

stuart briers

33 Eswyn Road
Tooting
London
SW17 8TR

t: 081 767 2618

Title
Weight Loss

Medium
Acrylic

Purpose of work
To accompany text

Brief
To reflect the text, i.e., the surgical removal of large amounts of body fat for primarily health reasons.

Commissioned by
Veronica Wadley,
Daily Telegraph

john brennan

34 The Cloisters
145 Commercial Street
London
E1 6EB

t: 071 247 1930

Title
Playing To Win

Medium
Acrylic

Purpose of work
Illustration for a weekly column in The Times Saturday Review

Brief
An open brief to illustrate a piece about the 'Foundation for Sport and the Arts', a body set up to form a linkage in funding between the two disciplines. The belief expressed in the piece was that the two do not mix.

Commissioned by
Chris Krage, Times Newspapers Limited

philip argent

1 Lupton Street
London
NW5 2JA

t: 071 267 8677

Title
Queen Elizabeth

Medium
Gouache and watercolour inks

Purpose of work
Cover of magazine

Brief
To illustrate the Queen for the 40th Anniversary of Accession cover, somehow depicting the length of her reign.

Commissioned by
Michael Rand,
Sunday Times Magazine

simon stern

19 Corringham Road
London N.W.11.

t: 081 458 8250

Title
The Sea-Change

Medium
Ink and watercolour

Purpose of work
Newspaper Illustration

Brief
Open brief to illustrate a review of "The Sea Changes" a book about the psychology of early emigrants to the U.S.A. and its effect on present day America.

Commissioned by
David Curless,
Times Saturday Review

nancy tolford

Studio 310
Panther House
38 Mount Pleasant
London
WC1X 0AP

t: 071 837 0509
081 800 3837

Title
GSM A Patchwork Quilt

Medium
Collage

Purpose of work
Magazine Article

Brief
For the next two years the Pan-European GSM Network will look more like a patchwork quilt than an evenly coloured blanket.

Commissioned by
Vincent Stokes, Harrington Kilbride

james marsh

21 Elms Road
London
SW4 9ER

t: 071 986 2441
f: 071 498 6851

Title
Birders of a feather

Medium
Acrylic on canvas board

Purpose of work
DPS in magazine

Brief
To illustrate feature article about the joys of bird watching.

Commissioned by
Suzanne Morris
Toronto Life Magazine

17

Work commissioned for advertising purposes appearing in newspapers, magazines and posters, advertising both products and events, but not personal promotion work.

Judges

Lesley Cobden	Ogilvy & Mather
Jo Gilson	DMB&B
Phil Howells	Still Price Lintas
Steve Long	Matthew Poppy Advertising
Tony Snow	Travis dale

ian reid parratt

Berkshire House
168/173 High Holborn
London
WC1V 7AA
t: 071 497 3575

Title
Ocean Friendly

Medium
Collage

Purpose of work
To advertise Ecover washing powder

Brief
Recycle old posters to make a poster to advertise Ecover (an environmentally friendly washing powder).

Commissioned by
Kiki Kendrick, Chiat Day

Client
Robin Bines, Ecover

kiki kendrick & keith bickel

Berkshire House
168/173 High Holborn
London
WC1V 7AA

t: 071 497 3575

Title
Mermaid

Medium
Collage

Purpose of work
To advertise Ecover washing powder

Brief
Recycle old posters to make a poster to advertise Ecover (an environmentally friendly washing powder).

Commissioned by
Kiki Kendrick,
Chiat Day

Client
Robin Bines, Ecover

rhonald blommestijn

Artbox
Krueslaan 182
1098 SK
Amsterdam
Holland
t: 31206681551

Title
Christmas Tree

Medium
Acrylic

Purpose of work
Adshel poster Brut

Brief
To create a surreal image incorporating the Brut Bottle in a Cnristmas scene.

Commissioned by
Phil Howells/Fianna Purcell, Still Price Lintas

Client
Elida Gibbs Limited, Brut

robin heighway-bury

The Drawing Room
Panther House
38 Mount Pleasant
London
WC1X 4OP

t: 071 833 1335
f: 071 837 6391

Agency
Spectron Artists

t: 071 240 2094
f: 071 240 2091

Title
Spaghetti 1

Medium
Pastel

Purpose of work
Billboard posters

Brief
To produce bold illustrations of well known Heinz products.

Commissioned By
Gerard Stamp, BSB Dorland

Client
HJ Heinz

unpublished professionals

Experimental work, personal promotion work, including speculative publishing proposals.

Judges

Paul Arrowsuch	Major Taylor Nicholson
Joanna Dale	Independent on Sunday Review
Peter Dyer	Jonathan Cape
Neil Littman	Pauffley & Co.
Anne Magill	Illustrator

tracy ramsdale

c/o Association of Illustrators
29 Bedford Square
London
WC1B 3EG

AOI
t: 071 636 4100

Title
Pandoras box

Medium
Lino cut and paper collage

paul hess

363B St. John Street
London
EC1V 4LB

t: 071 278 0724

Title
Gone Fishing

Medium
Watercolour

Purpose of work
Comment on 1992 General Election

paul hess

363B St. John Street
London
EC1V 4LB

t: 071 278 0724

Title
My Sister's Violin

Medium
Watercolour

Purpose of work
Book illustration

Brief
To illustrate a poem about the terrible standard of my sister's violin playing.

christina brimage

175 Choumert Road
London
SE15 4AW

t: 071 252 9354

Agent
Sharp Practice

t: 071 833 2564

Title
Wind Power

Medium
Gouache, collage

Purpose of work
Gold Awards Competition

Brief
To interpret the word 'Power'.

christina brimage

175 Choumert Road
London
SE15 4AW

t: 071 252 9354

Agent
Sharp Practice

t: 071 833 2564

Title
'Horse Power'

Medium
Ink, gouache, collage

Purpose of work
Gold Awards Competition

Brief
To interpret the word 'Power'.

janet woolley

34 Stanhope Road
London
N6 5NG

t: 081 341 3651

Title
Aries

Medium
Acrylic paint, montage

Brief
Experimental self-motivated work.

fletcher sibthorp

134 Salcott Road
London
SW11 6DG
t: 071 924 2473

Title
Gymnast Tryptich

Medium
Oil on canvas

Purpose of work
For the Gold Awards Competition.

Brief
To convey the word 'Power'.

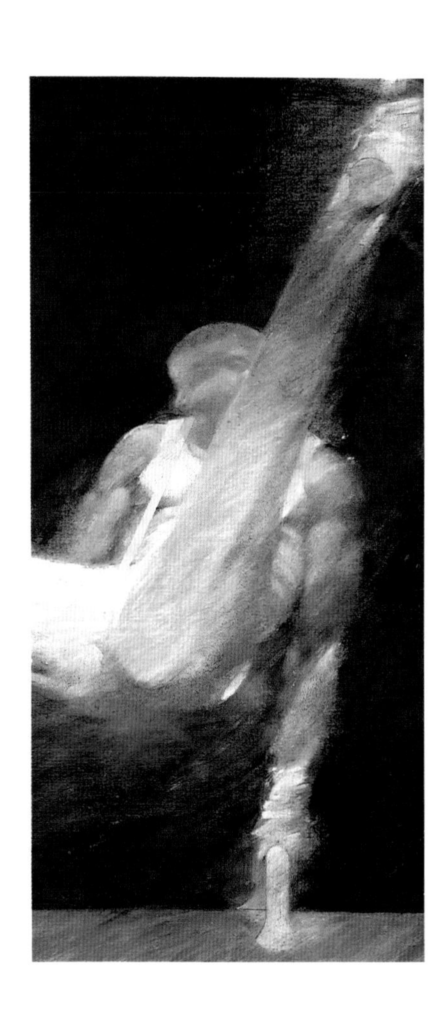

stephen pochin

21 Muswell Road
Muswell Hill
London
N10 2BJ

t: 081 883 2932

Title
"Log Basket Apostle Opium Denizens"

Medium
Computer generated photomontage

Purpose of work
Experimental Folio

Brief
To use computer paint programs to develop montage artwork that incorporates disparate iconic and textural material. A hybrid of the 'painterly' and the 'photographic'.

michael o'shaughnessy

The Organization
69 Caledonian Road
London
N7 9BT

t: 071 833 8268

Title
The Wire Walker

Medium
Watercolour and pastel

Purpose of work
Personal project

jane mccracken

25 Cargil Terrace
Edinburgh
EH5 3NF

t: 031 552 3917

Title
Untitled

Medium
Acrylic/Ink

Purpose of work
Personal work for portfolio

michael jackson

28 Tenham Avenue
Balham
London
SW2 4XR

t: 081 671 0085

Title
Blue Peter
Triptych"Shep's
First Photograph"

Medium
Screenprint

Purpose of work
Personal project

michael jackson

28 Tenham Avenue
Balham
London
SW2 4XR

t: 081 671 0085

Title
Blue Peter Triptych
"As soon as you're in the water get rid of as many clothes as possible"

Medium
Screenprint

Purpose of work
Personal project

michael jackson

28 Tenham Avenue
Balham
London
SW2 4XR

t: 081 671 0085

Title
Blue Peter
Triptych "Coylum
Marcus the £2,000
Champion Cat" clothes

Medium
Screenprint

Purpose of work
Personal project

elsa houghton

22 Battlefield Lane
Wombourne
Staffordshire
WV5 OJL

t: 0902 892662

Title
Time is But a Stream

Medium
Oil on paper

Purpose of work
College brief to produce an illustration for a calendar of literary quotations.

karen herring

75A Chestnut Grove
Balham
London
SW12 8JF

t: 081 675 7953

Title
Corbieres

Medium
Watercolour, bleach and pencil

Purpose of work
Self-promotion

Brief
To produce an illustration suitable for a wine label.

kevin hauff

99 Tregenna Avenue
South Harrow
Middlesex
HA2 8QP

t: 081 423 6486

Title
The Kipper Tie

Medium
Acrylic

Purpose of work
Experimental image

Brief
One of a series of experimental images taking a fashion icon and showing it being modelled by a "Fashion Dandy".

simon fell

87 Rothschild Road
London
W4 5NT
t: 081 994 6206

Title
Fruit Mountains

Medium
Colour copy and acrylic

Purpose of work
Speculative poster

james gosling

18 Winslade Road
Brixton
London
SW2 5JJ
t: 071 274 9726

Title
Untitled

Medium
Photocopy collage/emulsion on glass

Purpose of work
Self promotion

Brief
Series of works on the general theme of "Music".

james gosling

18 Winslade Road
Brixton
London
SW2 5JJ
t: 071 274 9726

Title
Music World

Medium
Acrylic on black sticky back plastic

Purpose of work
Self promotion

Brief
Series of works on the general theme of "Music".

helen clapcott

14 Crompton Road
Macclesfield
SK11 8DS
t: 0625 426205

Title
Row Upon Row Manchester

Medium
Tempera

paul burgess

73 Pascoe Road
Hither Green
London
SE13 5JE

t: 081 852 1600
f: 081 852 1600

Title
Fire, No. 23

Medium
Collage/gouache/photography/monoprint

Purpose of work
Experimental work

Brief
Series dealing with nature v technology

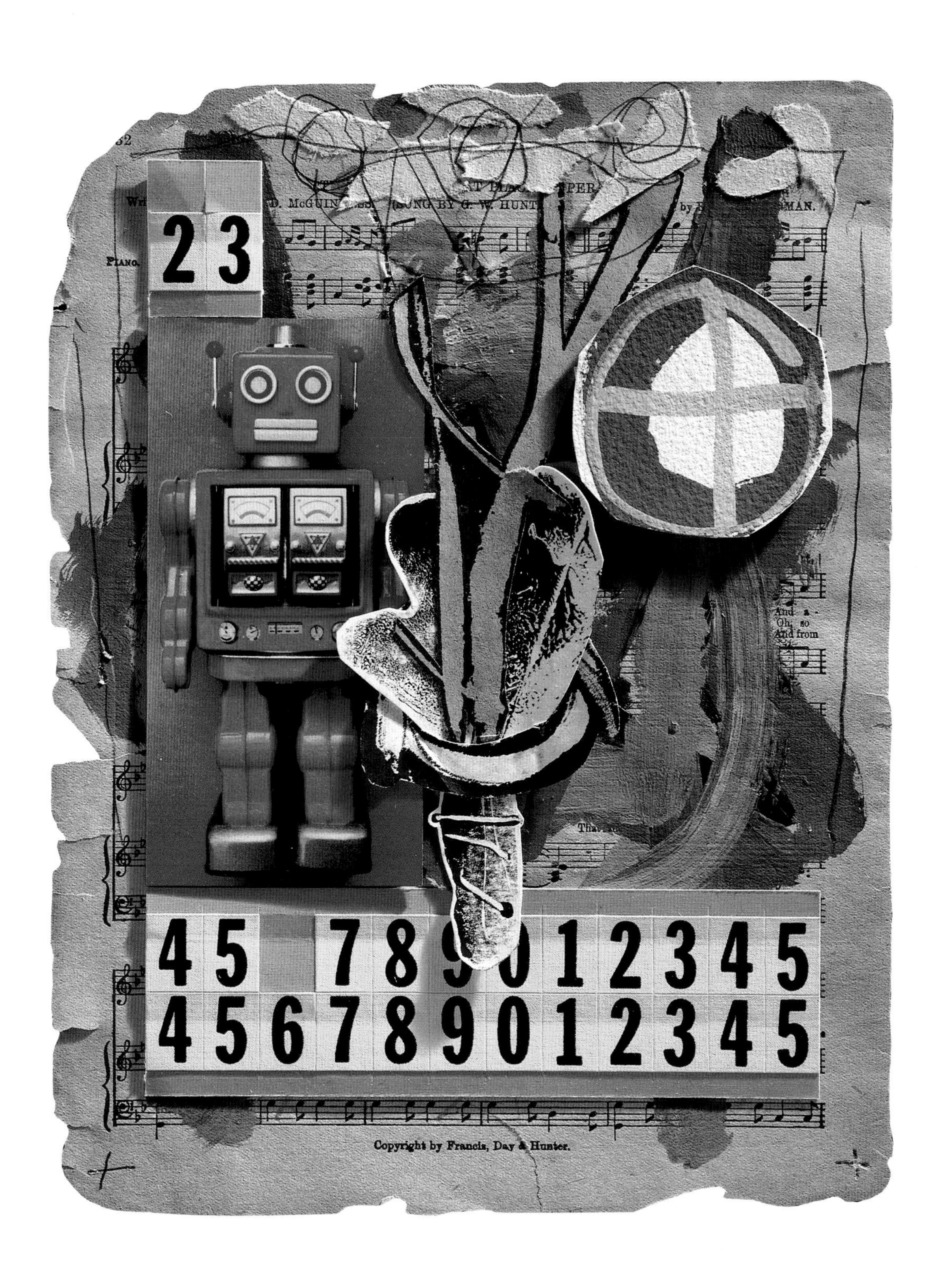

stuart briers

33 Eswyn Road
Tooting
London
SW17 8TR

t: 081 767 2618

Title
Figure/Forms

Medium
Acrylic

Purpose of work
Experimental

neil breeden

28 Vere Road
Brighton
BN1 4NR
t: 0273 686097

Title
Roses Have Thorns

Medium
Liquitex on wood panel

Purpose of work
Self promotional

michael bramman

104 Dudley Court
Upper Berkeley Street
London
W1H 7PJ

t: 071 723 3564

Title
In The Garden at No. 34

Medium
Acrylic

Purpose of work
Self promotional

michael bramman

104 Dudley Court
Upper Berkeley Street
London
W1H 7PJ

t: 071 723 3564

Title
Key West

Medium
Acrylic

Purpose of work
Self promotion

christian birmingham

t 0503 220484

Title
Brixton Market Fruit Seller

Medium
Alkyds

Purpose of work
Self promotion

ian mcfarlane

Fitch RS
Porters South
4 Crinan Street
London
N1 9UE

t: 071 278 7200

Title
Just Say Nein, You Burning Hunk of Funk

Medium
Sand blasted egg yolk on key fob

caroline della porta

Flat 3
22 Florence Road
Brighton
BN1 6DJ

t: 0273 554539
t: 0273 608102

Title
Outside Shibuya Station, Tokyo 29/9/91

Medium
Watercolour

Brief
To develop and record work on location

winners

unpublished student

Unpublished work executed by bona fide students

Judges

Julia Boulton	Living Magazine
Rydal Bowtell	Illustrator
Colin Brewster	New Scientist
Fiona Macmillan	Heinneman
Andrew Kingham	Illustrator

anna williams

179 Southgate Road
Islington
London
N1 3LE

t: 071 704 8691

Title
Sappho Enchants
The Sirens

Medium
Acrylic on Board

Purpose of work
Book Jacket

Brief
To illustrate the book jacket for a collection of short stories by Renee Vivien (personal project).

chris robson

7 Christina Terrace
Hotwells
Bristol
BS8 4QB

t: 0272 262620

Title
The Wheezing City

Medium
Acrylic

Purpose of work
Self set brief from magazine article

Brief
As the Wild West was being colonised, many hayfever and asthma sufferers moved to Tucson, Arizona, as the desert city was pollen free. The American desire for "suburbia" resulted in the planting of quick growing trees and lawns. Now, the pollen count has risen 35 fold and 70% of the population suffer from either hayfever or asthma.

georgios manoli

Kent Institute,
HND Graphics & Illust.
Oakwood Park
Maidstone
Kent
ME16 8AG

t: 0622 757286

Title
Who Knows Their Onions?

Medium
Acrylic on Canvas

Brief
To illustrate text
"Cry Out Against the Rampant Abuse of the Humble Onion".

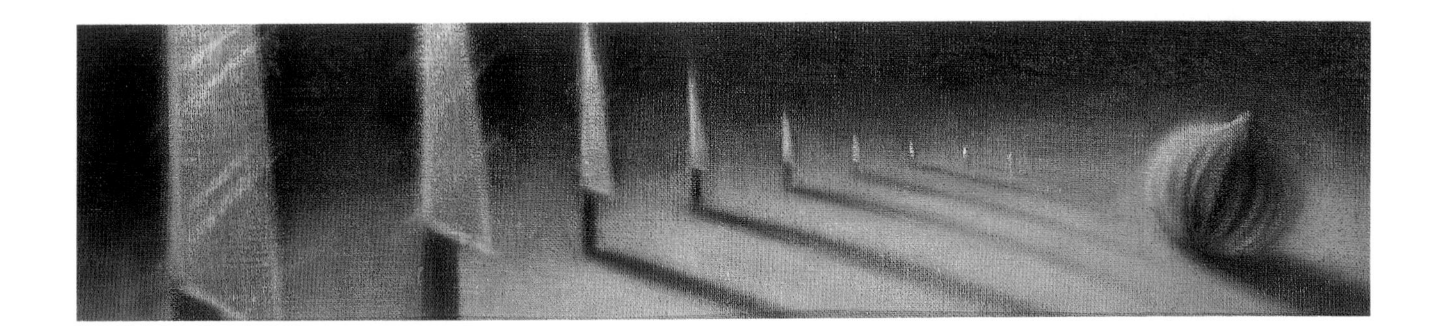

matthew macpherson

The Pales Cottage, LLandegley,
LLandrindod Wells, Powys,
LD1 5UH,
t: 0597 87543.

RGA School
Hane Bays
Sidcot School
Winscombe
Avon
BS25 1PD

Title
AIDS; The Disease is Spreading

Medium
Gouache on C.S.10

Brief
To produce an editorial illustration to accompany an article entitled "AIDS The Disease is Spreading" - Student project.

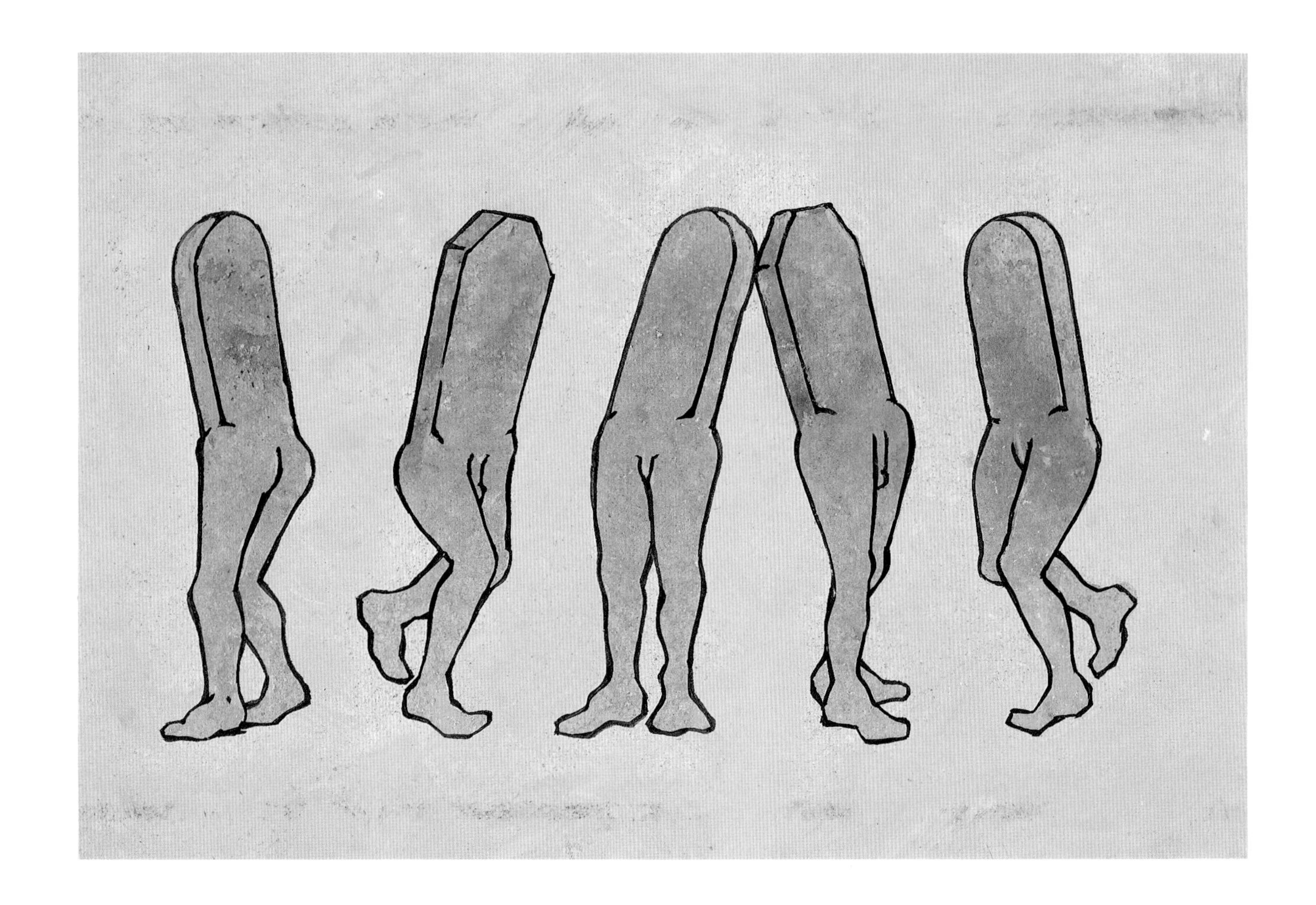

linda kent

34 Fieldgate Crescent
Birstall
Leicester
t: 0533 675478

Title
The Door

Medium
Etching, hand-made paper, acrylic inkwash

Purpose of work
Portfolio

Brief
Illustrate a number of poems from Ted Hughes' "Crow" with a view to producing a hand-made book as the finished artwork.

linda kent

34 Fieldgate Crescent
Birstall
Leicester

t: 0533 675478

Title
Robin Song

Medium
Etching, hand-made paper, acrylic and inkwash

Purpose of work
Portfolio

Brief
Illustrate a number of poems from Ted Hughes' "Crow" with a view to producing a hand-made book as the finished artwork.

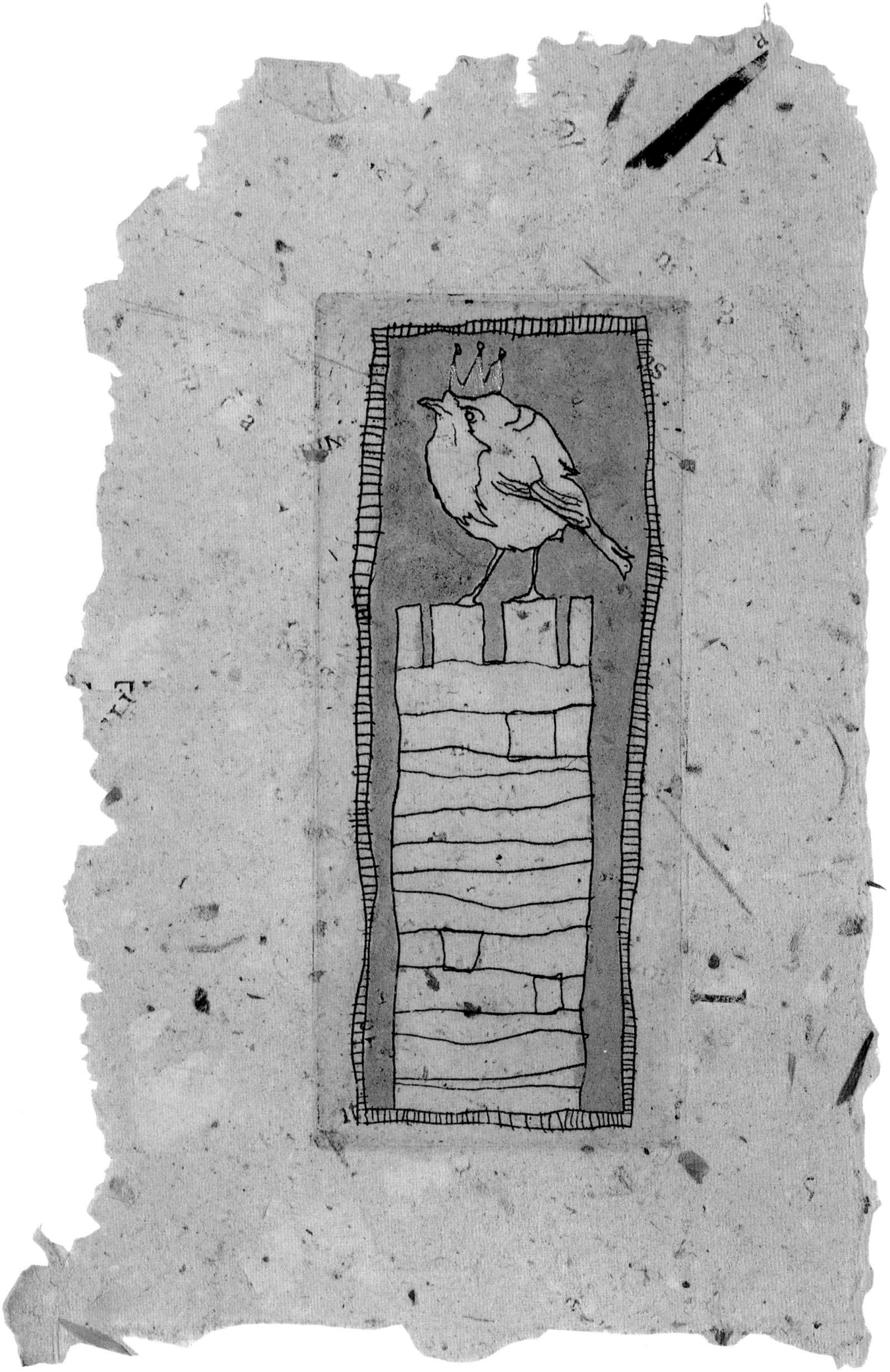

bruce cramp

The Patch
Lane End
Instow
Bideford
North Devon
EX39

Title
William 'N' Mary

Medium
Acrylic

Purpose of work
Book illustration

Brief
Produce an amusing image of William and Mary with reference to the Jacobite toast to the 'Little Gentleman in the Grey Waistcoat'.

martin cooper

Kent Institute of Art & Design
HND Graphics & Illustration
Oakwood Park
Maidstone
Kent
ME16 8HG

t: 0622 757286

37 Stanley Avenue
Dagenham
Essex
RM8 1JH

Title
The Big Apple

Medium
Acrylic on canvas

Purpose of work
College project

Brief
Illustrate an article on the return of traditional "old fashioned" apples to British shops.

104 Meadow Lane
Iffley Village
Oxford

OX4 4ED

t: 0863 772442

penny hardy

Title
The Tides

Medium
Black ink screenprint original

Purpose of work
An informative poster on the causes of the Earth's tides

Brief
To produce a poster aimed at adults and children to clearly and simply explain the reasons for the Earth's tides using illustrations and type to create a combined image.

marie fred dupre

237A North Street
Ashton Gate
Bristol
BS3 1JT

t: 0272 532879

Title
The Depressed Witch

Medium
Etching

Purpose of work
Children's book

Brief
The witch lost her cat Balthazar. He is her only friend so she has to get him back.

frazer lynden hudson

34 Priory Terrace
West Hampstead
London
NW6 4DH

t: 071 328 8100

Title
The Tempest · William Shakespeare

Medium
Pen and ink and wash on tinted water colour paper

Purpose of work
To illustrate William Shakespeare's Tempest

Brief
Produce illustrations to emphasise Shakespeare's Tempest.

frazer lyndon hudson

34 Priory Terrace
West Hampstead
London
NW6 4DH

t: 071 328 8100

Title
The Tempest · William Shakespeare

Medium
Pen and ink and wash on tinted water colour paper

Purpose of Work
To illustrate William Shakespeare's Tempest

Brief
Produce illustrations to emphasise Shakespeare's Tempest.

diane broadley

22 Westfield Park
Redland
Bristol
BS6 6LX

t: 0272 730370

Title
Aquarium

Medium
Oil pastel

Purpose of work
Poster promotion for new aquarium extension at Bristol Zoo.

samantha hignett

29 Bedford Square
London
WC1B 3EG
AOI
t: 071 636 4100

Title
"Ynys Enlli Sketchbook"

Medium
Watercolour and pencil

Purpose of work
Page from sketchbook/diary kept while living on an island off the coast of North Wales

Commissioned by
Project completed whilst a student at the Royal College of Art studying Natural History illustration.

winners

17

book

Work commissioned for books and book jackets including children's books

Judges

Dennis Barker	Arrow Books
Nick Castle	Harper Collins
Caz Hildebrand	Penguin
Liz Masters	Corgi
Clare Sleven	Longman

bee willey

32 Grove Road
London
E3 5AX
t: 081 981 4900

Title
The Ugly Sisters

Medium
Mixed media

Purpose of Work
Educational, English language children's book

Commissioned by
Mary Jane Wilkins, Letts

bee willey

32 Grove Road
London
E3 5AX

t: 081 981 4900

Title
Untitled

Medium
Mixed Media

Purpose of work
Educational, English language children's book

Commissioned by
Mary Jane Wilkins, Letts

doffy weir

116 Rushmore Road
London
E5 OEX
t: 081 836 1059

Title
There's A Monster
In My House

Medium
Watercolour

Purpose of work
A line of text 'She gets paint in her hair'

Commissioned by
Deborah Blackburn,
Collins Educational

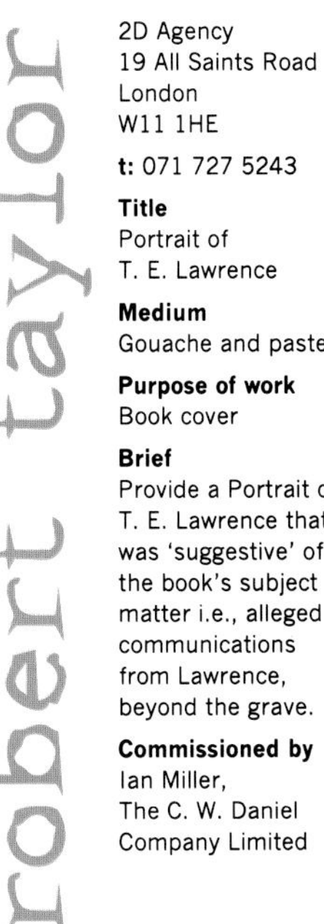

robert taylor

2D Agency
19 All Saints Road
London
W11 1HE

t: 071 727 5243

Title
Portrait of
T. E. Lawrence

Medium
Gouache and pastel

Purpose of work
Book cover

Brief
Provide a Portrait of T. E. Lawrence that was 'suggestive' of the book's subject matter i.e., alleged communications from Lawrence, beyond the grave.

Commissioned by
Ian Miller,
The C. W. Daniel
Company Limited

susan sluglett

155 Trellick Tower
Golborne Road
London
W10 5UT

t: 081 968 8077

Title
The Elected Member

Medium
Chalk pastel

Purpose of work
Book jacket

Brief
To give a taste of the story including the main character of the book.

Commissioned by
Peter Cotton, Abacus

sue williams

Agency
Folio
10 Gate Street
Lincoln's Inn Fields
London
WC2 A3HP
t: 071 242 9562

Title
The Great Rain

Medium
Pastel coloured crayon

Purpose of work
Illustration of native American legend for childrens picture book 'Time for Telling'.

Brief
Copy was given for 15 stories from around the world with their roots in a spoken tradition, now written down.

Commissioned by
Karen Gray, Jackie Dobbyn

Client
Grisewood and Dempsey
Kingfisher Books

sarah perkins

37E Guiness Court
Snowfields
London
SE1 3SX

t: 071 378 1510

Title
Love in the Time of Cholera

Medium
Mixed

Purpose of work
Book jacket for Gabriel Garcia Marque

Brief
Read the novel

Commissioned by
Peter Dyer,
Johnathan Cape

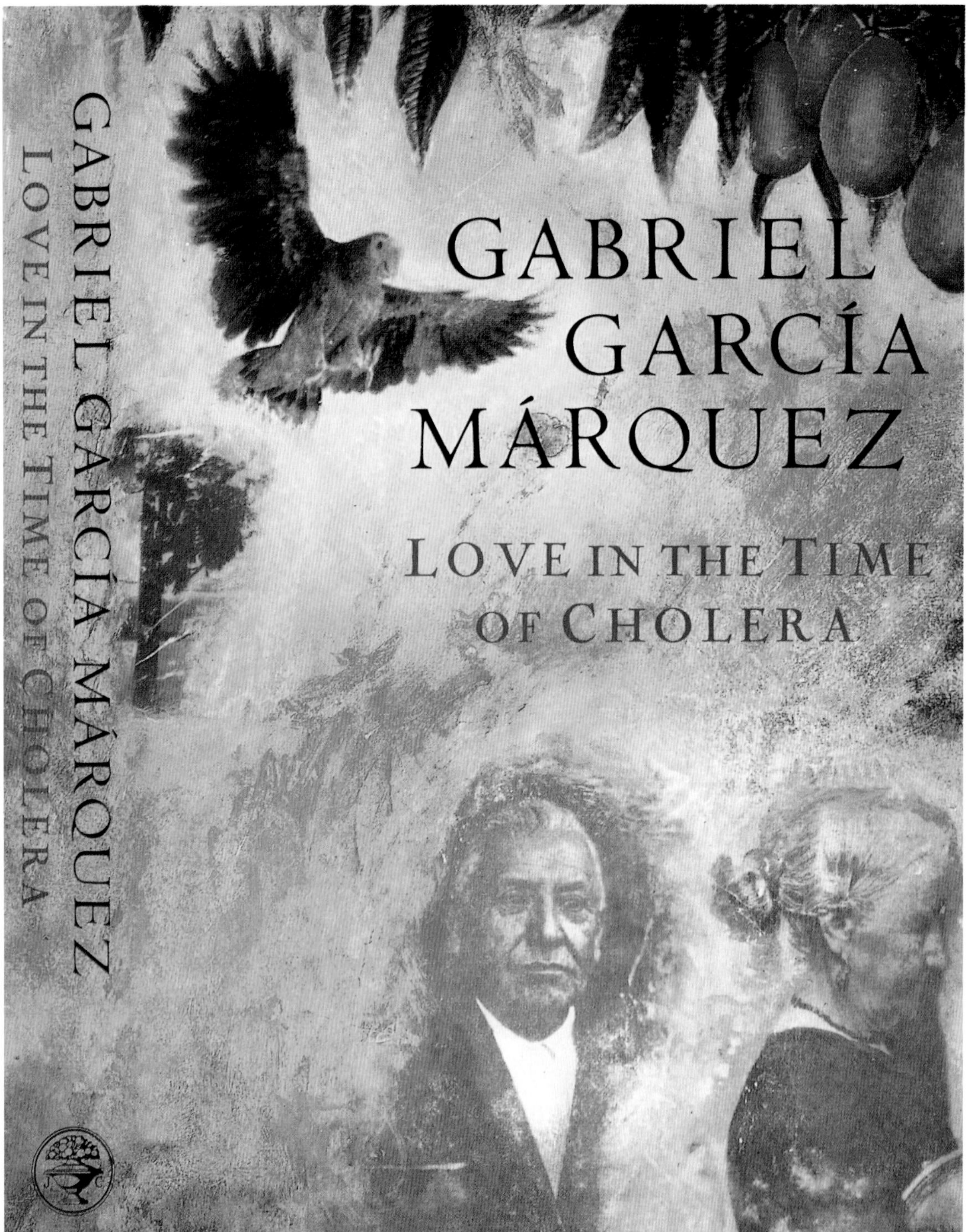

sarah perkins

37E Guiness Court
Snowfields
London
SE1 3SX

t: 071 378 1510

Title
In Evil Hour

Medium
Mixed

Purpose of work
Book Jacket for Gabriel Garcia Marque

Brief
Read the novel

Commissioned by
Peter Dyer,
Johnathan Cape

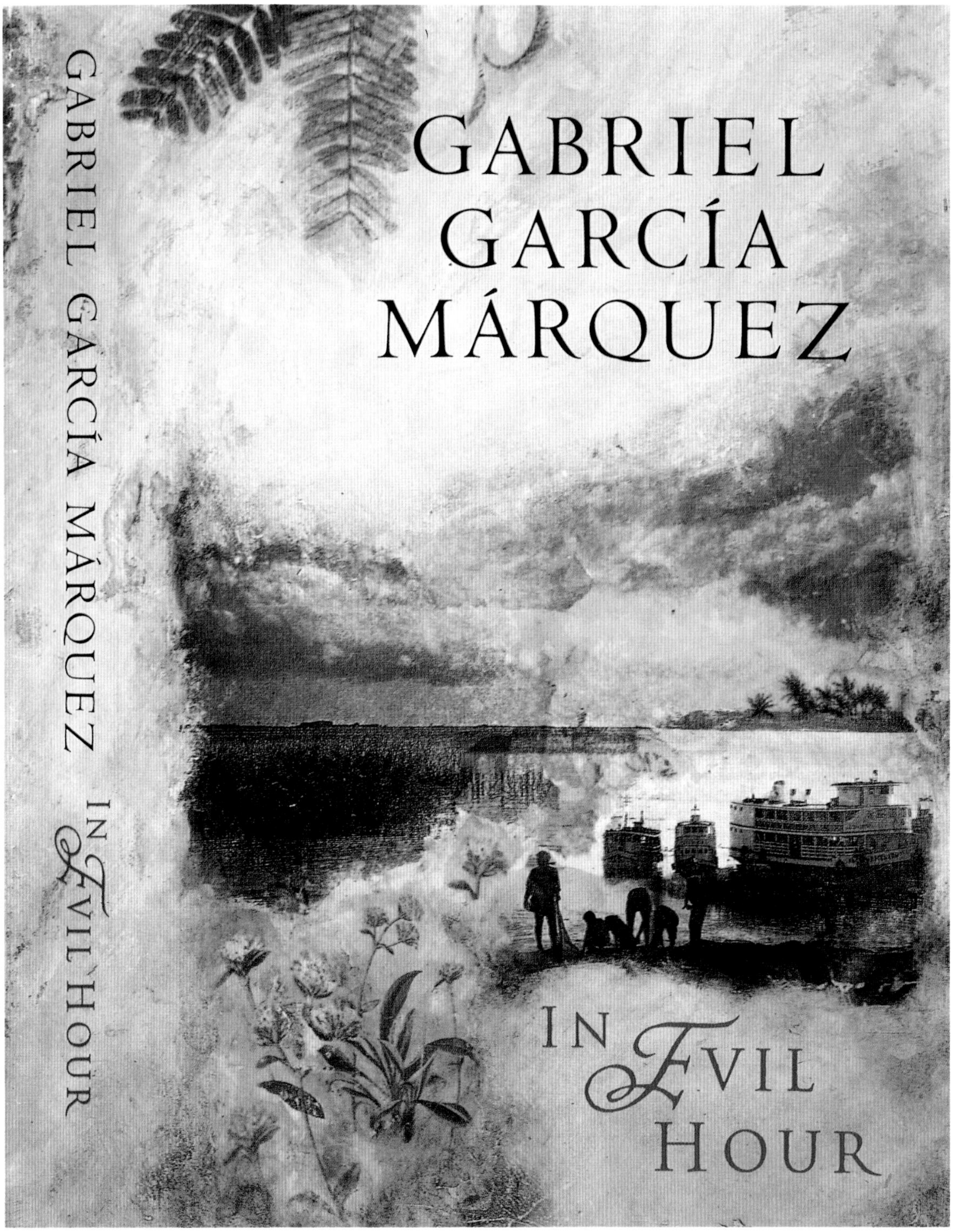

GABRIEL GARCÍA MÁRQUEZ

GABRIEL GARCÍA MÁRQUEZ

IN EVIL HOUR

IN EVIL HOUR

frances myers

Elsley Court
20-22 Gt Titchfield St
London
W1

t: 071 436 5681

Title
The Nepalese
Paper Book

Medium
Mixed Media

Purpose of work
To demonstrate the versatility and uses of paper

Brief
A visually stunning
and interesting way of presenting paper in all its different forms and uses from bank notes to flying pigs to ancient forms of suffocation.

Commissioned by
Frances Myers,
The Body Shop Design Team

21 Elms Road
London
SW4 9ER

t: 071 622 9530
f: 071 498 6851

Title
Fox Tales

Medium
Acrylic on canvas board

Purpose of Work
Book cover

Brief
Open brief · to include a fox, for this collection of foxy stories.

Commissioned by
Rosemary Summerhays,
Arrow Books

andrew davidson

Moors Cottage
Swells Hill
Burleigh
Stroud
Gloucestershire
GL5 2SP

t: 0453 884650

Title
The Battle

Medium
Wood engraving

Purpose of work
Complete book

Brief
Illustrate the story of Wistman's Wood and the Mink Wars.

Commissioned by
Janice Thomson,
Faber & Faber

andrew davidson

Moors Cottage
Swells Hill
Burleigh
Stroud
Gloucestershire
GL5 2SP

t: 0453 884650

Title
The Undoing

Medium
Wood engraving

Purpose of work
Complete Book

Brief
Illustrate the story of Wistman's Wood and the Mink Wars.

Commissioned by
Janice Thomson,
Faber & Faber

john bradley

10 Gate Street
Lincoln's Inn Fields
London
WC2A 3HP

t: 071 242 9562

Title
Losthearts #2

Medium
Ink, collage

Purpose of Work
Book "Mostly Ghostly"

Brief
Illustrate the story

Commissioned by
Nicholas Dawe, Folio

anne magill

Talberg Illustration
142A Greenwich High Road
London
SE10

t: 081 293 1304

Title
Summer Rain

Medium
Acrylic

Purpose of Work
Book jacket

Brief
To illustrate after reading manuscript

Commissioned by
Andrew Evans,
Harper Collins

Karisma

Karisma, the fine arts division of Berol Limited, produces an unparalleled range comprising: pens, lead pencils, markers and its award winning coloured pencils.

Karisma, soft leaded, coloured pencils are of the finest quality, with 108 striking colours and unique formulation, providing artists with the most comprehensive professional range available.

Osmiroid

Osmiroid produces quality fountain and calligraphy pens, designed to suit all ages and abilities.

Its extensive range of competitively priced calligraphy products ensure that beautiful handwriting is only a pen stroke away!

Contact:
Roger Young
European Marketing Manager
Berol Limited
Oldmedow Road
King's Lynn
Norfolk PE30 4JR
Tel: 0553 761221 Fax: 0553 766534

Professionals

paulene doyle

Studio:
12 Flitcroft Street
London
WC2H 8DJ

t: 071 240 4587
f: 071 240 3517

Home
t: 071 482 6036

Clients in 1992 include
Redwood Publishing, Emap Metro, GE Publishing, IPC, Aim Publications, Emap Elan, International Thompson Publishing Limited, Harrington Kilbride PLC, Shaws Publications, Fleetway Editions, GAT Publishing, International Magazines Limited, The Health Education Authority, etc..

c/o Central Illustration
Agency
36 Wellington Street
London
WC2E 7BD

t: 071 240 8925
f: 071 836 1177

Since the beginning of his career, Brian Grimwood has consistently attracted the most prestigious commissions in advertising and design. As well as working for all the major advertising agencies, design groups and publishing houses in the U.K., he also regularly receives commissions from clients in Europe, the Far East and the USA.

jean-paul tibbles

c/o Central Illustration Agency
36 Wellington Street
London
WC2E 7BD

t: 071 240 8925
f: 071 836 1177

This portrait of Inge Huibregtse is one of many commissioned portraits produced alongside work for major advertising agencies, design groups and publishers.

edward briant

c/o Central Illustration Agency
36 Wellington Street
London
WC2E 7BD

t: 071 240 8925
f: 071 836 1177

Edward Briant has worked extensively in Britain and the United States over the last ten years. His clients have included: The New York Times, Swissair, Pentagram, Lloyds Bank, The Scottish Health Authority and The Rough Guides.

belinda richards

c/o Central Illustration
Agency
36 Wellington Street
London
WC2E 7BD

t: 071 240 8925
f: 071 836 1177

Since leaving Brighton Polytechnic in 1988, I have worked on a large variety of jobs within publishing and design. Clients have included The Penguin Group, Sunday Times, The Post Office, Lewis Moberly, Safeway, Tesco, Alliance and Leicester and Ian Logan Design. I enjoy working mainly in Oil Pastel, but love mixing different media and collage.

claire davies

c/o Central Illustration Agency
36 Wellington Street
London
WC2E 7BD

t: 071 240 8925
f: 071 836 1177

Claire Davies has worked for numerous design groups and publishers, including Boots, Sainsburys, Penguin, MacMillan Publishing, Pan and various European packaging designers.

brian sanders

c/o Central Illustration Agency
36 Wellington Street
London
WC2E 7BD

t: 071 240 8925
f: 071 836 1177

These paintings were commissioned on behalf of The Marshal Islands by Unicover USA, as part of a six year 'History of World War II in Postage Stamps' that the artist is currently working on.

Each painting is designed to crop to a pair of se-tenant stamps and by bisection to provide a 1st Day Cover cachet for each stamp.

paul burgess

73 Pascoe Road
London
SE13 5JE

t: 081 852 1600
f: 081 852 1600

Collage/3-D mixed media illustration. Work has been featured on television, book covers, record sleeves and appears regularly in the National Press.

Previous clients include
Island Records, Jonathan Cape, MTV, The Guardian, The Independent, The Observer, The Times, Telegraph Magazine, and New Scientist. Recent Exhibitions: 'Art in Boxes' England & Company, 3-Dimensional Illustrators, New York.

peter warner

Boundary View
Hillside Road
Tatsfield
Westerham
Kent
TN16 2NH

t: 0959 577270
f: 0959 541414

Milka cow for Suchard billboard campaign in France promoting a new Lila Pause strawberry bar. Strawberries were added to either head or horns to go with witty play-on-words captions. The cow - in two poses - had to look soft, feminine, proud, knowing and mischievous; and still so 200 faxes - but not hours - later!

bill butcher

43 Coronet Street
London
N1 6HD
t: 071 729 9184
f: 071 739 9558

One of a series of illustrations, commissioned by The Times Saturday Review, in favour of steering heavy goods traffic off the highways and on to the railways.

neil hague

176A Merton High
Street
Wimbledon
London
SW19 1AY

t: 081 543 2217
f: 081 540 0416

My inspiration comes from everything from Marc Chagall's work to Native American Indian sand paintings and from space adventures to 'Watch with Mother'. I work in gouache using bold and bright colour or black and white, combining dream-like qualities with a cartoon feel.

Recent clients include
The New Statesman and Society, VNU Business Publications, Centaur Communications , BBC Radio Times, The Builder Group PLC, London Borough of Merton, A.I.R. Theatre Group, S.P.L. Design and Quartet Books Limited.

chris burke

76 Auckland Road
Tunbridge Wells
Kent
TN1 2HS

t: 0892 531329
f: 0892 531329

Chris Burke has been an illustrator since 1984. He has contributed to The Sunday Times, The Radio Times, Punch, Campaign, The Guardian, etc. He has won awards for his work for The Irish Tourist Board and the Creative Circle Gold Award for illustration for his work for Save The Children.

alan young

2 Chapel Cottages
Dunks Green
Tonbridge
Kent
TN11 9SF

t: 0732 810652

"Firelight". Illustration for a short story in Lear's Magazine, New York, art director: Bruce Ramsay. Alan Young's illustration has been published in Canada, USA, Europe, as well as in the UK.

satoshi kambayashi

c/o Ian Fleming & Associates Limited
No 1 Wedgwood Mews
12/13 Greek Street
London
W1V 5LW

t: 071 734 8701
f: 071 439 3400

Graphic Humorist
Cartoons, humorous and conceptual illustration.

Clients
Punch (1987-1992), The Spectator, Die Welt, Hor Zu, The Saturday Evening Post, The Japan Festival, Heinemann International.

Other Reference
Art '93

cyrus deboo

7 Copse Wood
Iver Heath
Buckinghamshire
SL0 0PT

t: 0753 651104

pauline hazelwood

38 Mayfield Avenue
Southgate
London
N14 6DU

t: 081 886 7833
f: 081 886 6812

I enjoy working on humorous subjects. Past clients include: J Sainsbury, TVS, JWT, Walker Books, Scholastic. I also work in black and white.

oliver burston

52 Barbauld Road
London
N16 0ST

t: 071 254 2856
f: 071 241 6049

Recent clients include
Barclays Bank, IBM, BMW, Unilever, HMSO, United Distillers, Peat Marwick McLintock, Transport Mutual Insurance, TSB, United Newspapers, The Design Council, The Body Shop, World Travel Markets, Wiggins Teape Papers, Student Travel Association, Genesis Travel, Manchester City Olympic Bid, Penguin Publishers, You Magazine, Octopus Publishers.

maggie sawkins

82 Highbury New Park
London
N5 2DJ

t: 071 359 0160

Illustration for Ideal Home, Sticks and Stones, item on bullying. I aim to convey the essence of a brief through the energetic use of gestural figures and colour.

Clients include
Addison, Amnesty International, Centaur, Emap Elan, Hot Graphics, IPC, Redwood.

dan davis

176 Dover House Road
London
SW15 5AR

t: 081 878 0651

Clients include
Paul Weller and The Style Council (Confessions of a Pop Group), Billy Bragg, Viscountess Rothermere, The Times, Director Magazine and various trade magazines. In 1987 I won second prize in The Benson and Hedges Gold Awards and in 1990 I won The Beresford Sherman Award for best unpublished work, Images 15, and this elephant was drawn out of pure mischief!

julia heseldon

12 Stroyan Street
Burnley
Lancashire
BB10 4DP
t: 0282 25011 Ex 2562
Home
t: 0282 53132
f: 0282 55464

Versatile artist with many different styles ranging from detailed product shots to loose watercolours, decorative fresh and feminine, also detailed natural history/ botanical subjects. Work can be seen on Marks & Spencer and Boots product ranges.

Work experience includes designs for ceramic transfers, book covers for World International and CO-OP, greetings cards for Aries, Hambledon Studios, CCA Stationery and Henry Ling & Company.

julia midgley

140 Chester Road
Northwich
Cheshire
CW8 4AW

t: 0606 781490
f: 0606 781490

Julia Midgley lives and works in the North West. Her work is included in numerous public, private and corporate collections. Increasingly she has become involved with corporate art, working with industry in the work place and on the factory floor.

Clients include
Ocean Transport & Trading, I.C.I., Shell U.K., Rothschilds PLC, AMEC PLC, Trafalgar House, Rickitt & Mitchell, Syltone PLC, Cheshire County Council.

murray zanoni

9 Park Lane
Woodstock
Oxfordshire
OX20 1UD

t: 0993 811347

Clients have included
American Express, British Telecom, Cathay Pacific Airlines, The Design Council of Great Britain, Illustrated London News, Penguin Books, The Sunday Times and Wines from Spain.

Has travelled extensively to produce portfolios of work on a wide range of places and subjects.

(Illustration from a portfolio of Watercolours and Drawings on Macau).

sally brewer

270 Guildford Road
Bisley
Woking
Surrey
GU24 9AF

t: 0483 475682

Title
Guildford High Street.

Medium
Watercolour and pencil.

Graduated Kingston Polytechnic 1989.

Work profile
Architectural and food illustrations for magazines including BBC Good Food, Homes and Gardens, and Sunday Express Magazine. Also work for hotel publicity, travel brochures and guides (Time Off Limited, AA/Thomas Cook), illustrated maps, golf club brochures, and children's educational publications for Oxford University Press.

jacky rough

142 Gledhow Wood Rd
Leeds
West Yorkshire
LS8 1PF

t: 0532 667985

My work is mainly figurative: from bold and cheerful crayon compositions to graphic pen and ink designs suitable for printing in two or more colours. Plenty of movement and pattern. See also Contact 5, 6, 7, 8 and The Creative Handbook 1993.

Top left and right
From the booklet accompanying each packet of 'Livial - Sympton Relief after the Menopause'. Commissioned by Simon Brown Press & Public Relations for Organon Laboratories Limited.

Below
Commissioned by the Girl Guides Association for 'The Official Guide Annual 1993'.

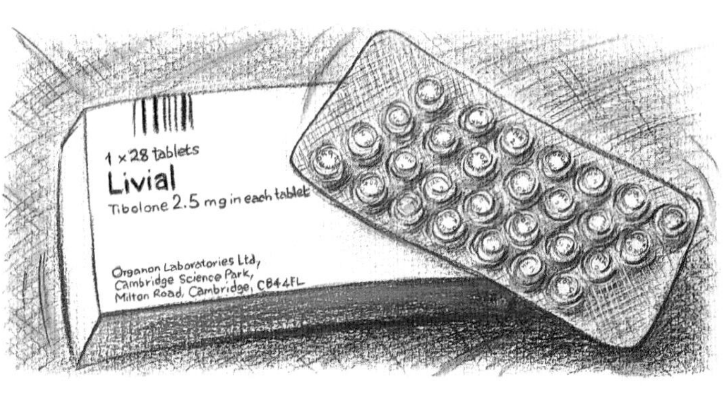

annabel wilson

35 Aldensley Road
London
W6 0DH
t: 081 741 8876

Annabel offers the services of illustration and visualisation of buildings and interiors. The work is executed in watercolour or black and white line and wash.

Recent commissions include
Illustrations of Hampton Court Palace and gardens, brochure illustrations for Tarmac Properties and Speyhawk PLC, and the London Ark at Hammersmith. The majority of her current work is carried out to commission for interior designers and architects. She is able to work from architects drawings and plans to realise the illustration.

72 Highburgh Road
Glasgow
Scotland
G12 9EN

t: 041 334 4265

Although I am essentially a portrait painter, my work has been used in magazine articles and for book illustrations. This watercolour portrait was commissioned by Mrs. Paul-Fox for her daughter's 21st birthday. The portrait was designed to illustrate Bridget's youth, confidence, potential and her ability to cope with future challenges. I wanted to keep the atmosphere light, airy and natural.

mario minichiello

61 Scotland Road
Little Bowden
Market Harborough
LE16 8AY

t: 0858 431456
f: 0858 431456

I have worked in all fields of illustration and for national and international clients. I work quickly when required and I enjoy solving design problems. I recently enjoyed a long term commission from The Guardian newspaper working with Micheal Pilgrim.

Recent clients include
Graphic Direction, BBC Publications, World Publication and various one-off commissions for newspapers and magazines.

anton kazlauciunas

12 Victoria Cottages
Off Deal Street
London
E1 5AJ

t: 071 377 9072

A pre-budget 1992 drawing for The Guardian's weekly 'Platform;' page. Article headlined 'A Chance to be Chancellor' and written by five economists of varying persuasions, giving their views on what Mr. Lamont ought to do and what they expected him to do.

martin jones

Warren House
Blundellsands Road
West Merseyside
L23 6TF
t: 051 924 5160

Clients include
Geographical Cover, Marketing Week Cover, Times Educational Supplement, Nursing Times, Director and Redwood Publishing.
See also *Images 15*.

gini wade

Plas Tylwch
Tylwch
Llanidloes
Powys
SY18 6JN
t: 059788 627

Illustration from "The Wonderful Bag" (Blackie 1993). Other clients include: Pan/MacMillan, Julian McRae Books, Oxford University Press, Orchard Books, Octopus Books, M.G.P., Folens, Ginns, etc..

151 Wensleydale
Terrace
Blyth
Northumberland
NE24 3HF

t: 0670 356299

david mitcheson

Specialising in figurative work in watercolour and acrylic. Working for a broad range of clients in editorial, advertising, book and packaging design.

Illustration shown
"The Color Purple". Commissioned by Philip Atkins for the Cambridge University Press.

stephen jeffrey

Talberg Illustration
142A Greenwich High Road
London
SE10

t: 081 293 1304
f: 081 293 1268

80 Finsbury Avenue
Newcastle Upon Tyne
NE6 4BR

t: 091 276 0667

Top
Client, H.H.L. for Marketing Business. The Threat to Telesales Businesses, Posed by European Legislation.

Bottom
Client, New Scientist. The Battle against Restrictive Practises within the Medical Establishment.

The Function of Illustration is to clarify and delight, I see this as essentially a design problem. At the heart of this 'problem' is the balance between the specific and the general, the mundane and the universal. Illustration is an angel in overalls.

paul campion

30 Hayesford Park Drive
Bromley
Kent
BR2 9DB

t: 081 464 2067
f: 081 464 2067

What other famous artists have said about Paul Campion. "Not as good as me!" · Andy Warhol. "Two cucumbers and a light bulb" · Salvador Dali. "He's a bit nifty with the old airbrush" · Leonardo Da Vinci. "Who?" · Pablo Picasso.

26 Alma Road
Penylan
Cardiff
CF2 5BD

t: 0222 493432
f: 0222 493432

Benson and Hedges Gold Awards 1989 and 1991 highly commended. European Illustration 1990/91. 1991 Magazine Publisher's Awards best front cover - business section. Samples - T.S.B.: tiered interest rates. Radio Times: the guilty party. Director: get rich/stay small. As well as finished artwork - I also work as image consultant - faxing concept visuals to your design brief for your illustrator/ photographer to stylise.

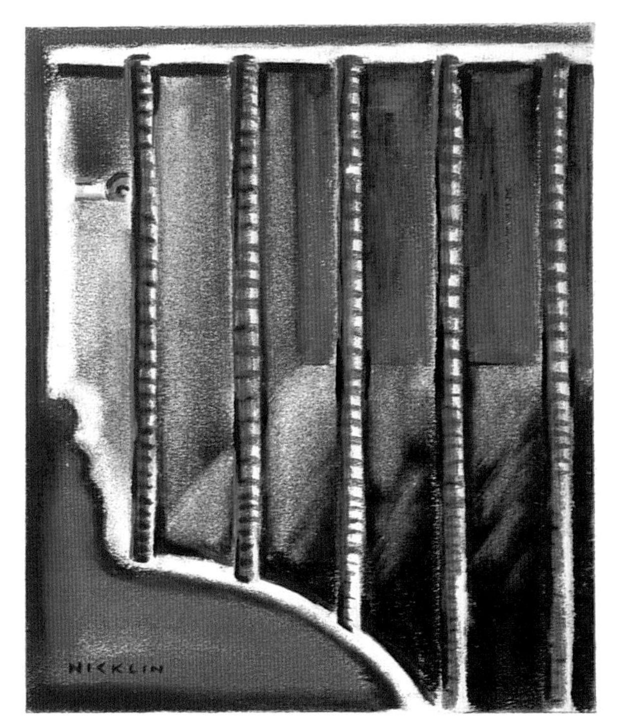

bekah o'neill

25 Ampton Street
London
WC1X 0LT
t: 071 837 2931

Medium
Collage

My work has been used by a variety of clients including - MacMillan Magazines, Serpents Tail, Emap Women's Group, Headway Hone & Law Publishing, IPC Magazines and Redwood Publishing. Illustration shown here, for Lotus Magazine.

mollie picken

The Old Post Office
Sibford Gower
Banbury
Oxfordshire
OX15 5RT

t: 029 578629

Illustration work includes
'Love and Marriage', Christine Bloxham and Mollie Picken, published Webb and Bower 1990. Colour, black and white illustrations throughout form vital and integral part of book. Hunkydory Designs published Christmas Cards 1991. Drawings, diagrams for Textile Books Published: Studio Vista, BT Batsford, Herbert Press, David and Charles. 'Embroidery Studio' PSG Embroiderers' Guild to be published David and Charles 1993. Oxfordshire Museum Services, 'Cogges Farm House Kitchen' small recipe book based 1900 illustrations throughout, colour separations, page layouts.

angela caunce

43 Berkshire Drive
Congleton
Cheshire
CW12 1SB

t: 0260 270088

Self promotion
Little Bo Peep. Airbrushed 200 x 285mm.

felicity roma bowers

Roseland
38 Bailbrook Lane
Bath
BA1 7AN

Home
t: 0225 313301

Studio
t: 0225 425135

Penguin, Bodley Head, Gollancz, Heinneman, OUP, CUP, Radio Times, British Rail, Holland & Barratt, and W. H. Smiths are some of the clients who have used my work. Also this year, cover for album and singles for Genesis and packaging for Marks & Spencer. I work with watercolour, pastel and tissue paper collage, mixing media to achieve the rich colours and textures I enjoy. I aim for atmosphere and enjoy contributing as much as possible to the creative ideas process.

david atkinson

19 Battledean Road
Highbury
London
N5 1UX

t: 071 359 3271
0249 715870

Line drawing for Annabelle Magazine (Zurich). Art Director: Beni Dittli. Headline: Schon Wie Adonis (Beautiful as Adonis). Copy: On men going to beauty clinics/ narcissism/hedonism/ beauty. Who's it for? The beautified or the observer. Drawn images that illustrate and explain but also ask questions.

hazel brook

18-20 Prospect Place
Hastings
East Sussex
TN34 1LN
t: 0424 443541
f: 0424 443541

I have had a number of illustrations published for various clients, including Design Groups, Health Authorities and Local Government. I have exhibited in various exhibitions including two recent exhibitions at the Association of Illustrators Gallery and have undertaken several public art commissions in vitreous enamel, including sixteen murals for the Isle of Dogs Neighbourhood Centre and a mural for a public library in Eastbourne. I am particularly interested in commissions for environmental groups, editorial and book illustration.

caroline e porter

Garden Studio
Flat 1
No. 65 Carleton Road
London
N7 0ET

t: 071 607 8128
f: 071 700 1688

Brief
2 bookjacket covers from a series of phrasebooks, aimed at the younger market. The images were to convey the atmosphere and enjoyment of a holiday as well as recognisable aspects of the country being visited.

Commissioned by
Amanda Hawkes

Client
Hodder & Stoughton

eric beaumont

83 Prince George Road
Stoke Newington
London
N16 8DL

t: 071 249 4753

Title
The Gardener (1992)

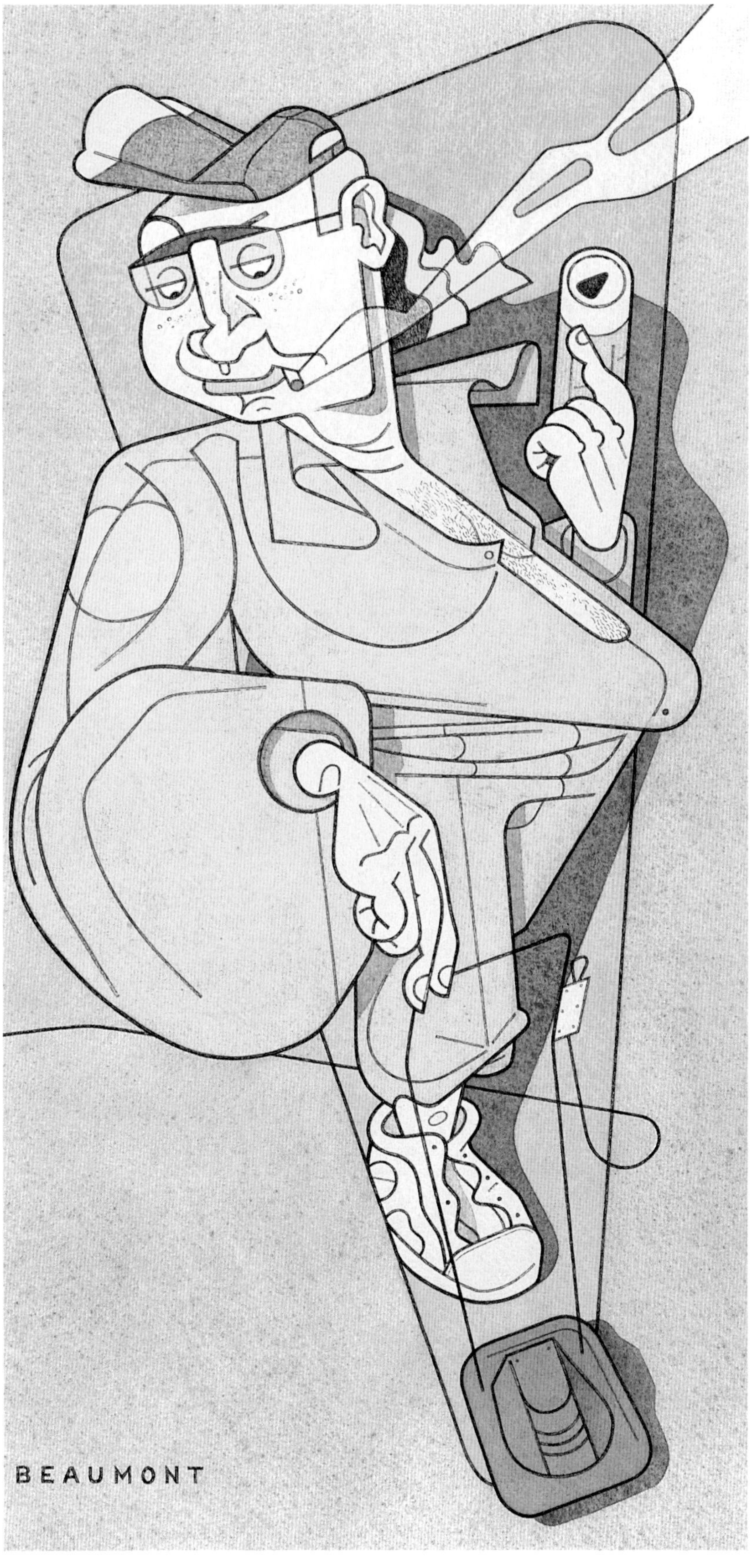

dave wood

8 Pickering Rake
Sefton
Bootle
Merseyside
L30 0PR

t: 051 924 2527
f: 051 924 2527

Unlike buses my work turns up on time! I produce illustrations to fit your brief and your deadline! The image below is just one example of my new style, which is proving to be very rewarding. If you want to know if I can illustrate more than bus-stops, then phone me for a broadsheet or a personal portfolio presentation.

Clients include
Ziff Davis Ltd., The Item Group, Financial Times Magazines, The Binding Brown Partnership.

melanie bowles

Studio 353
27 Clerkenwell Close
London
EC1 QAT

t: 071 251 3470
f: 071 490 0063

One of a series of food illustrations

Past clients include
Din Associates, David Davies Associates, Michael Peters, The Chase, Still Waters Run Deep, Athena International, Cosmopolitan, Chemistry Britain, Nicole Fahri, You Magazine.

tim gravestock

35 Loates Lane
Watford
Herts
WD1 2PE

t: 0923 252460
f: 0923 254644

Title
Kenting

Medium
Mixed Media

Client
HHL Publishing

Art Director
Bev Douglas

Brief
DPS illustration to accompany article about Kenting National Park in Taiwan.

andrew fowler

593 London Road
Earley
Reading
Berkshire
RG6 1AT

t: 0734 267800

Speculative work for a CD cover for 'La Mer' by Claude Debussey. Mixed media piece comprising ink, linoprint and collage.

helen j holroyd

Providence Studio
3-4 Ann Street
Brighton
BN1 4GP

Studio
t: 0273 676640
f: 0273 690628

Home
t: 0273 696681

Original, distinctive and reliable editorial, design, publishing and advertising.

Clients include
Oxford University Press, Thomas Nelson and Sons Publishers, Sunday Times, Observer, Radio Times, Redwood Publishing, Twocan Publishing, Esquire, Body Shop and lots of design groups.

carla miles

40 Sycamore Road
Shinfield
Reading
Berkshire
RG2 7YL

Title
Mountains and valleys

Client
Tia Maria

Publication
Special promotions brochure.

One of a series of illustrations depicting a variety of coffee growing regions.

t:0734 752812

jake abrams

Talberg Illustration
142A Greenwich High Road
London
SE10

t: 081 293 1304
f: 081 293 1268

Editorial, advertising and design illustrations.
Please ring to view folder.

jon hamilton

207B Chevening Road
Queens Park
London
NW6 6DT

t: 081 968 7481

I photograph all my work myself, supplying a high quality 5x4 transparency, and provide detailed line drawing roughs. Work is produced in a short space of time.

Clients
British Telecom, J Walter Thompson, Chiat Day, Royal Academy of Arts, Conran Design , Jonatahn Cape.

'Empty promises', illustrating an article on support services provided by software companies for Micro Decision magazine.

'Portrait of Isaac Newton', illustrating an article on scientists and the constants they discovered. Apples reflecting Newton's discovery of gravity, are real. for New Scientist magazine.

curtis tappenden

4 Winchester Street
Brighton
East Sussex
BN1 4NX

t: 0273 600246

The image shown here was recently commissioned by The Mail on Sunday newspaper for a promotional feature in conjunction with The Royal Academy of Arts. The brief was to present Academy President, Sir Roger de Grey and selected elements of Burlington House to the newspaper readership in a realistic but fresh way. Like much of my work it was executed within a very tight deadline.

Clients include
Reed Publishing, Country Homes & Interiors, Homes & Gardens, Richard's Bicycle Books, The Mail on Sunday.

martin orme

c/o 29 Bedford Road
Macclesfield
Cheshire
SK11 8JG

t: 0625 614201

The brief shown was to take the traditional English story of Jack and the Beanstalk and to interpret it in a decorative and dynamic way. Recent commissions have included; illustrations for an Irish Heritage video, packaging of Co-op 99 Tea, a poster for Tetley's brewery, greetings cards and ceramic transfers.

Although I live and work in Manchester a move of house is imminent. Please get my present contact from the listed address.

paul davis

Home
t: 071 289 3684

Studio
t: 071 247 7603

Agency
Debut Art

t: 071 254 2856
f: 071 241 6049

Top
Listen carefully
(televisual)

Bottom left
Communication
(unpublished)

Bottom right
The effect of
microgravity on
molecules
(New Scientist)

Many editorial, design and advertising commissions including, Virgin, Warner Bros., Barclays, Olivetti, American Express, MTV, Random Century, IPC, Unilever, Centaur, BP.

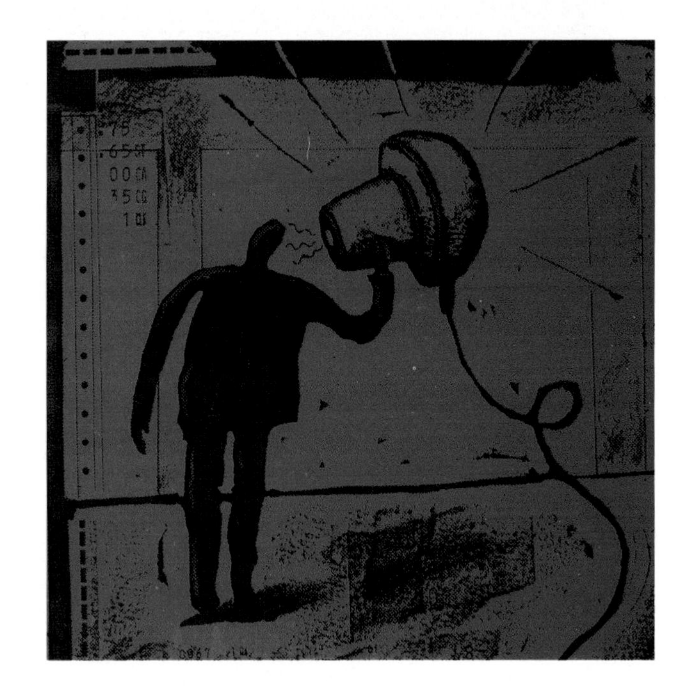

nick maland

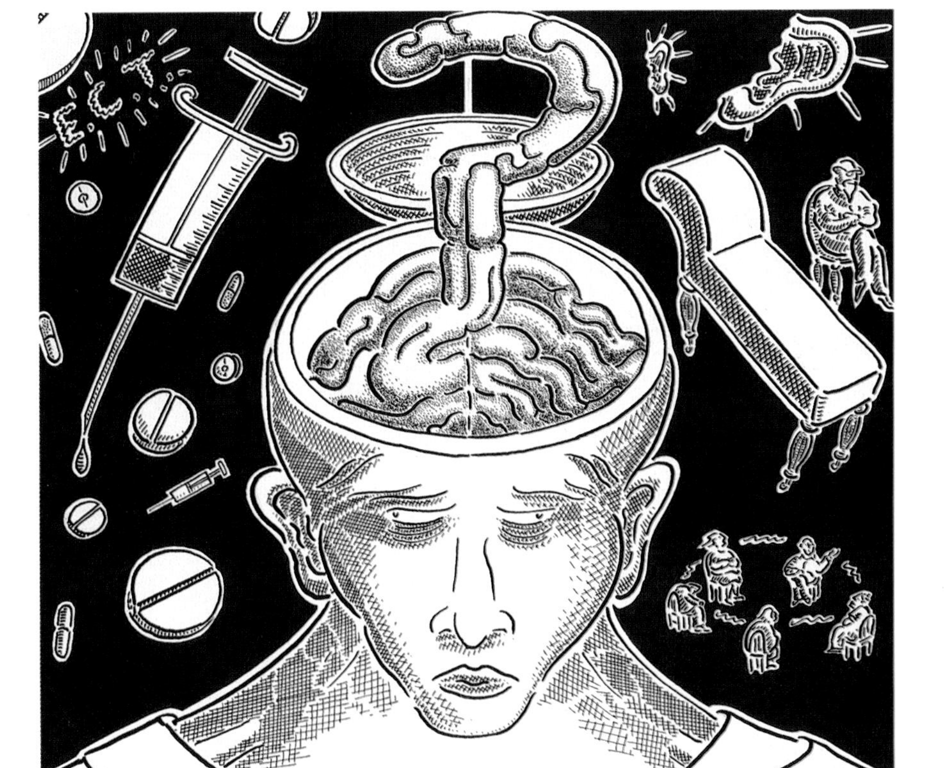

t: 071 286 3634

Recent clients include
The Times,
The Financial Times,
The Guardian,
The Observer,
The Independent etc..

Top
Physiology versus
Psychology
The Times

Bottom
Minding your P's
and Q's · The Times

rachel chilton

8B Grove Park
Camberwell
London
SE5 8LR

Studio
t: 071 274 6401

Home
t: 071 274 1735

I work in both mixed media/collage and lino.

Clients include
The Independent on Sunday, Jonathan Cape, Marshall Cavendish, Mitchell Beazley, Penguin Books, Perception Design, The Symington Company, The Observer.

simon henwood

t: 081 806 0744

Agency
Gotham Art and Literary Agency Inc.
New York

t: 212 989 2737
f: 212 645 7731

UK clients include
Pan Books, Macmillan, Collins, Oxford University Press, The Bodley Head, Linguaphone, National Magazine Co., etc..

US clients include
Farra, Straus and Giroux, The Putnam and Grosset Group, William Morrow, Atheneum, Simon and Schuster, The New York Times, etc..

All illustrations from 'The Hidden Jungle', published by Farra Straus and Giroux.

john townend

Studio 332
Stratford Workshops
Burford Road
Stratford
London
E15 2SP

t: 081 519 4512
f: 081 503 0390

My background is in industrial design and now drawing architectural, landscape and transport subjects freely plein-air is my speciality also in watercolour pastel and oil paints. Work recently published by Quarto in the encyclopedia of coloured pencil techniques. Member of AOI and ACG Arts Centre Group.

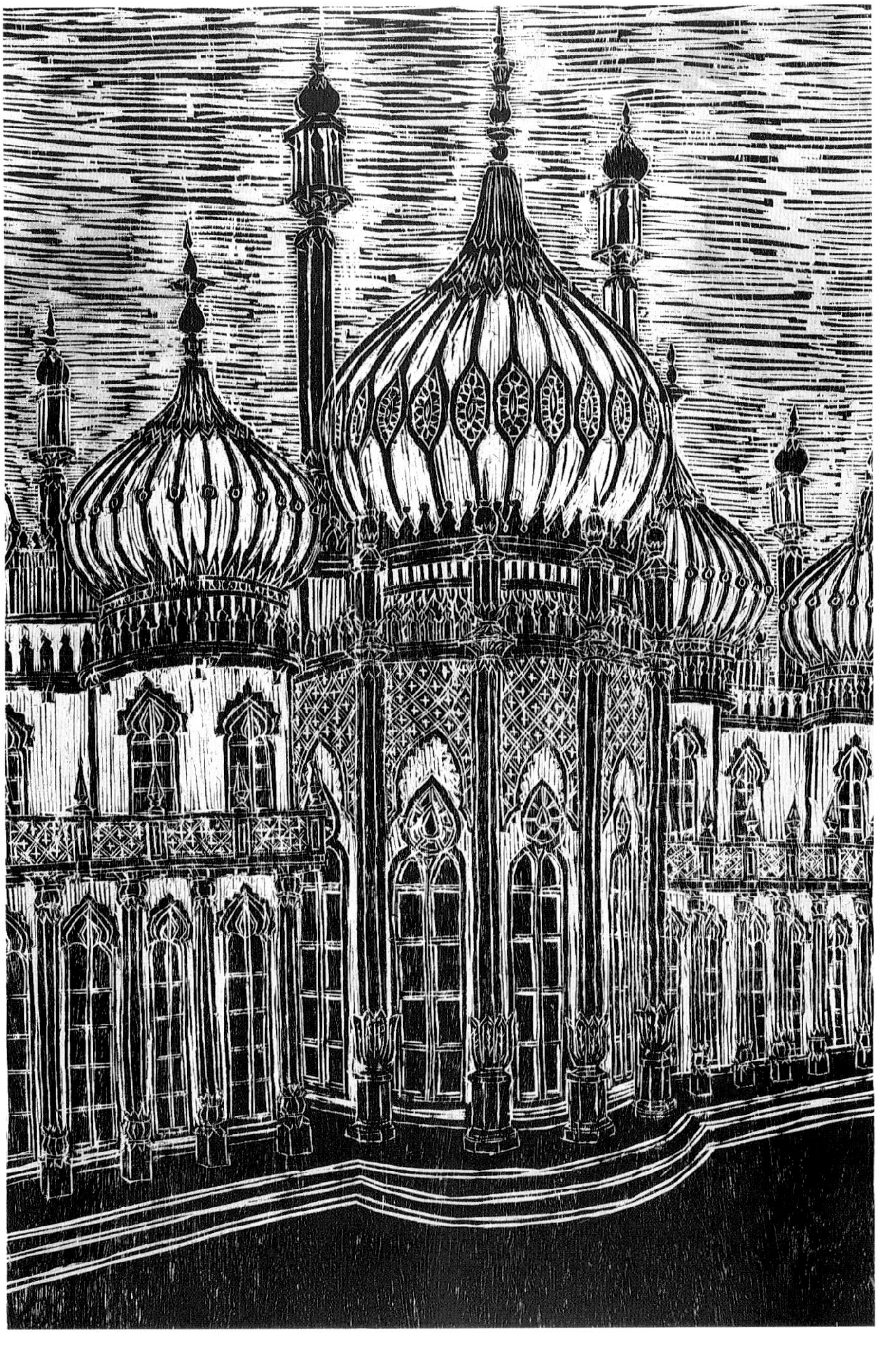

caroline bilson

Manor Farm
Little Addington
Kettering
Northants
NN14 4AY

t: 0933 650744
f: 0933 650744

Woodcut of Royal Pavilion made into posters for Brighton Council to sell in the Brighton Centre, Royal Pavilion Shop and Brighton Museum Shop.

Mainly architectural/ travel illustration in a variety of media, pen and wash, woodcut, linocut, scraperboard etc..

Clients include
British Rail, Hodder & Stoughton, First Leisure Corporation, Oxford University Press, TSB, Ernst & Young, Coopers & Lybrand Deloitte, Brent Walker Breweries, Trafalger House.

toby morison

Big Orange
2nd Floor
Back Building
150 Curtain Road
London
EC2A 3AR

t: 071 739 7765
f: 071 613 2341

Article entitled 'Intelligent buildings'

Medium
Acrylic on sugar paper

Commissioned by
Angela Poston, Human Resources Magazine
Howson and Leach Publishing

BIG ORANGE is a group of illustrators working from a studio in Shoreditch, London.

andrew lovell

Big Orange
2nd Floor
Back Building
150 Curtain Road
London
EC2A 3AR

t: 071 739 7765
f: 071 613 2341

Cover 'Night geometry and Garscadden Trains' by AL Kennedy

Medium
Printmaking, collage and photocopying

Commissioned by
Sedley Place Limited

Published by
Phoenix

jason ford

Big Orange
2nd Floor
Back Building
150 Curtain Road
London
EC2A 3AR

t: 071 739 7765
f: 071 613 2341

Title
Fido reads skull wrestler

Medium
Acrylic and ink on board

Unpublished from a solo exhibition held in Tokyo, Japan, in April 1992 with sponsorship from the British Council.

sarah mcmeneny

Big Orange
2nd Floor
Back Building
150 Curtain Road
London
EC2A 3AR

t: 071 739 7765
f: 071 613 2341

Title
Archway, Florence 1992

Unpublished

Medium
Mixed media

dan williams

Big Orange
2nd Floor
Back Building
150 Curtain Road
London
EC2A 3AR
t: 071 739 7765
f: 071 613 2341

Article entitled 'Aristocrats'

Commissioned by
GQ Magazine, May 1992
Conde Nast Publishing

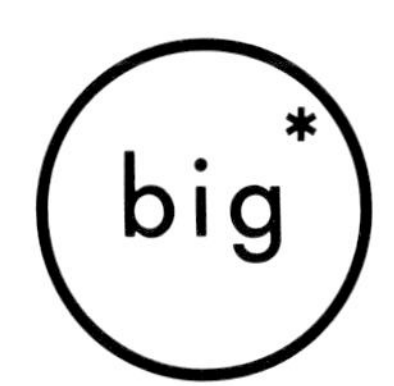

jane human

Big Orange
2nd Floor
Back Building
150 Curtain Road
London
EC2A 3AR

t: 071 739 7765
f: 071 613 2341

Unpublished

Medium
Oil on paper

lawrence zeegen

Big Orange
2nd Floor
Back Building
150 Curtain Road
London
EC2A 3AR

t: 071 739 7765
f: 071 613 2341

Title
Father's day 1992

Medium
Silkscreen print

Commissioned by
New York Card Company

rod vass

81 Torbay Road
London
NW6 7DT

t: 071 372 6840
f: 071 372 0684

Clients include
Amusement Business, BBC, British Airways, British Rail, Centaur, Coca-Cola, Commercial Union, Disney, Fleetway, Gerry Anderson, Guinness, Halifax, Harper Collins, Hill Samuel, Home Office, Honda, IBm, IPC, JVC, Kodak, Longmans, Lyons, MacDonalds, Marlboro, Marvel, Mecca, Mentorn, Michael Joseph, Michelin, Mirrorsoft, OUP, Peugeot, Precision Marketing, Procter & Gamble, Publitek, Royal Mail, Showerings, TSB, Virgin, Western Union, Wrigleys.

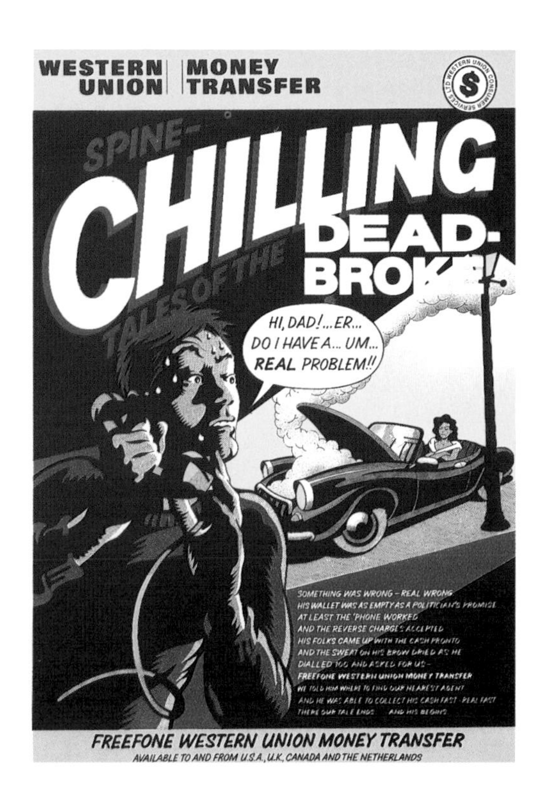

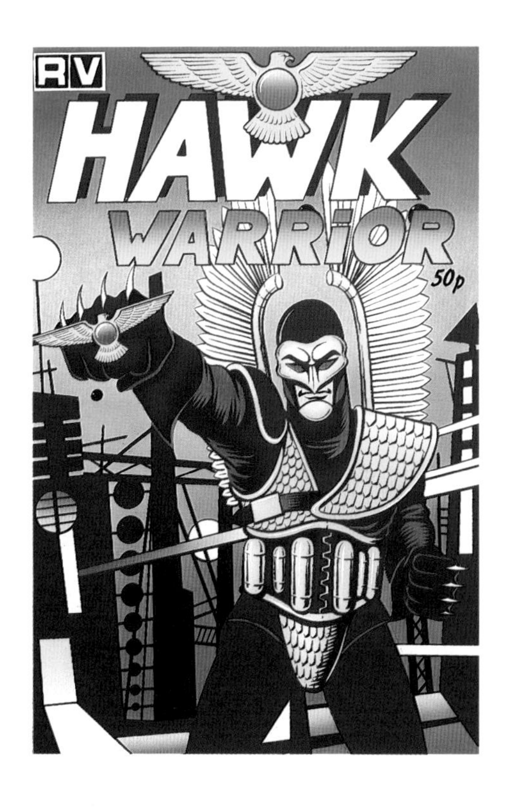

13mg TA
SMOKIN
Health Departments

·1mg NICOTINE
AUSES CANCER
hief Medical Officers

1 Church Crescent
London
E9 7DH
t: 081 986 5589
f: 081 986 5589

annemarie huck

newcomers

17

sarah g lees

Caeau Newydd
Milo Llandybie
Rhydaman
Dyfed

SA18 3LZ

t: 0269 831241

Freelance Wildlife Illustrator

Illustration
Tropical Fish

Medium
Watercolour and oil pastel

sarah j coleman

6 Hays Lane
Hinckley
Leicestershire
LE10 0LA

t: 0455 635125

I am always intrigued by the places where writers choose to write. Completed early in my second year at Birmingham Polytechnic, this image illustrated a passage by PD James. Turn the page upside down - the picture can be viewed in any direction!

More recent work has included the manipulation of fabrics, surface and texture, metallics and beads - a kind of two dimensional recycling system and something I'd like to expand on after graduation in 1993. 33 weeks and counting!

shook sam

41 Adeney Close
Hammersmith
London
W6 8ET
t: 071 386 7326

Graduated from Bath College of Higher Education in the Summer of 1991. Illustration was commissioned by 'Image Processing' magazine to illustrate the idea of the paperless office by introducing Document Image Processing (DIP) Systems.

juliet winters

The Old School House
Compton Dando
Pensford
Bristol
BS18 2JZ

t: 0761 490821
f: 0272 541158

peter arnold

129 Mickleburgh Hill
Herne Bay
Kent
CT6 6JZ

t: 0227 369256
f: 0227 364421

The illustration is an published editorial project for promotional purposes. The article reads "Gold cards, are they worth their weight in plastic?" and examines the benefits available such as holiday medical insurance, discounted car hire and cheaper hotel booking and considers if the expensive fees are worthwhile. I am an experienced graduate illustrator with published work in my folio and currently looking to branch into design and advertising work.

mandy cox

37 Sandford
Ringwood
Hants.
BH24 3BZ

t: 0425 474509

One of a series illustrating the Alan Bennett Talking Heads Plays this one is taken from 'A Chip in the Sugar'.

richard jenkins

26 Lindore Road
Battersea
London
SW11 1HJ

t: 071 223 3296

Clients
Random Century Publishing, Serpents Tail Publishing, Harrington Kilbride Publishing, Gaia Books Limited, New Woman Magazine, Screen International, Haymarket Publishing Services Limited, Black Spring Publishing, Sedley Place Design.

Image One
New Woman Magazine

Image Two
Serpents Tail Publishing

mikey georgeson

Rosetta Studios
36 Great Russell Street
London
WC1B 3PP

t: 071 637 7245
f: 071 436 5338

Illustration Title
"Migraine"

mary stubberfield

c/o 16 Buckhurst Close
Eastbourne
East Sussex
BN20 9EF

t: 0323 508697

My distinctive style concentrates on a strong use of colour. Subjects include architecture, animals and food, often incorporating decorative borders.

Clients include the English Tourist Board, Co-op Supermarket, You Magazine and Athena. This image is in inks and bleach, commissioned by Just 17 Magazine. It illustrates a short story titled 'The Date'.

Agent
London Art Collection

t: 071 376 7773
f: 071 376 7576

susie louis

c/o A.O.I.
Bedford Square
London
WC1B 3EG
t: 071 636 4100 (A.I.O.)

Self-generated brief theme - perfect portraits. Computer generated image. Clients - English Tourist Board, NIM, NIM Musik, City Bank, World Runners and Youth Ending Hunger.

tony heap

29 St. Augustines
Crescent
Chesterfield
Derbyshire
S40 2SG

t: 0246 207951
f: 0246 207951

Top
One of a set of four self-promotional postage stamps based on the theme 'Summer'. Lino-cut 12 x 16.4cm.

Bottom
Self promotional illustration to accompany an article on the Virtues of Lobster, for a food and drink editorial. Lino-cut 26.5 x 25cm.

Commissions to date have been in the areas of advertising, packaging and design.

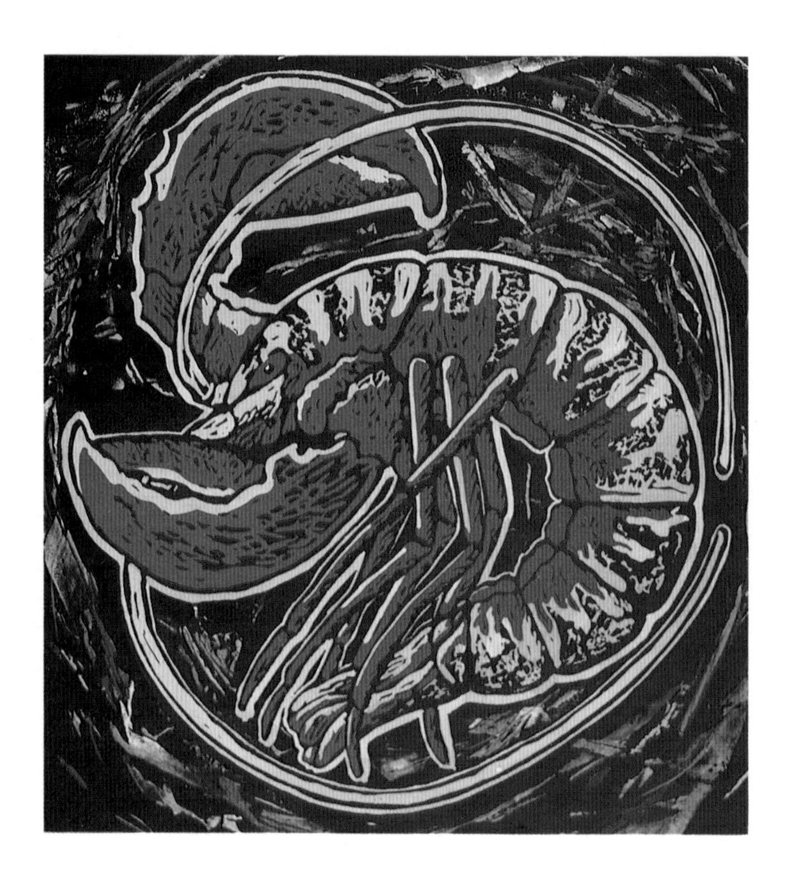

37 Stanley Avenue
Dagenham
Essex
RM8 1JH

t: 081 595 3388

Title
Working Together

Client
Eurotunnel/Kent Institute of Art & Design.

Brief
The Brief was to produce an illustration for the 1993 Eurotunnel calendar, based on the theme of linking Britain more closely to continental Europe. It was set in the form of a competition for which this illustration won the Brown Knight & Truscott Young Designer of the Year Award.

margaret welbank

52C Mansfield Road
London
NW3 2HT

t: 071 267 8658

Illustrator/cartoonist with a background as a psychologist in industry and an eye for movement and expression. Special skill in creating humorous but informative illustrations on technical, business and educational subjects. Major recent projects include: illustrating a manual on training design (ICI); story, text and illustrations for a comic book introduction to System Dynamics (BP); also illustrations to Merryweathers on the Moon and Mum's Big Secret (Letts Educational) and a variety of other educational publishing and editorial commissions.

david ryan

44 Oxleay Road
Rayners Lane
Harrow
HA2 9UY

t: 081 429 0934

Title
Political Power (The Manipulation of the Electorate).

The basis of my work is to stimulate thought, and questioning of the subject illustrated. Underlying most of my work are influences from literary subjects, also I try to project myself and humorous elements to produce figuratively interesting images.

henning lohlein

237A North Street
Bristol
BS3 1JJ

t: 0272 532879

Clients include
The Observer Magazine, BBC Holidays, Design Week, Dennis Publishing.

Top Left
Poster Competition "The New Generation of Europeans"

Top Right
Illustrated French Proverb "You Don't Win Much By Running Around The World". (Most French spend their holidays in their own country).

Bottom Left
Cover for Design Week

Bottom Right
Illustration of the Parisian Public Transport System

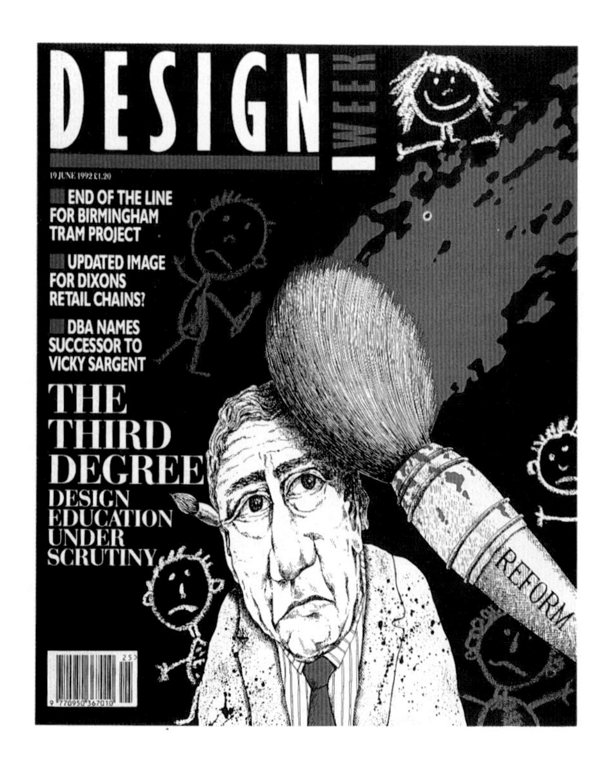

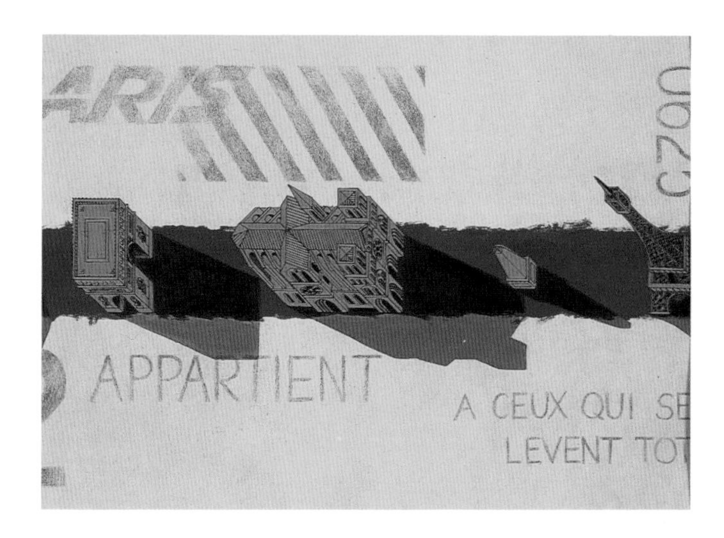

keely mitchell

5 Hichisson Road
London
SE15 3AN

t: 071 732 6905
f: 071 603 2890

Title
'Tipping the Balance'.
A winning entry in the 1992 illustration competition to celebrate Oxfams 50th Anniversary: 'It's Time For A Fairer World', organised by Oxfam and the Association of Illustrators.

rachel baker

5 New Cottages
Deenethorpe
Nr. Corby
Northants
NN17 3EP

t: 078085 345

I work mainly in acrylics on textured backgrounds in my own personal style. This is contemporary, while being semi-representational and combines realism with a distinctive image. Black and white or colour is equally effective. I was awarded a highly commended prize in the Benson and Hedges Illustration Gold Awards 1991. The illustration shown is entitled "Telly Addicts".

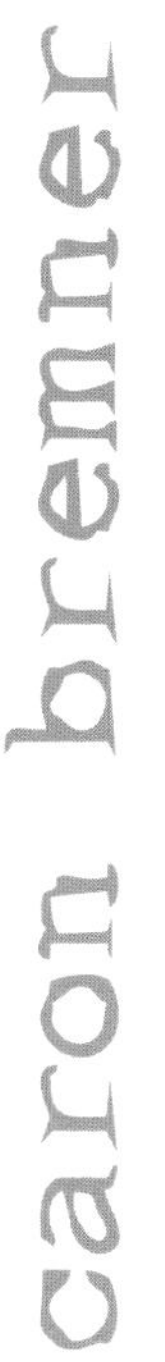

14 Stable View
Yateley
Camberley
Surrey
GU17 7SF

t: 0252 872763

Title
Three Worlds As One.

Brief
The idea was to show the first, second, and third world countries working as one, showing they could benefit each other. For use as a poster for charity.

Currently a student at Brighton Polytechnic.

paula knight

11 Ambrose Road
Clifton Wood
Bristol.
BS8 4RJ

t: 0272 265757

Clients
Bristol Community Festival; W.O.M.A.D.; N.M. Lighting. Subject Matter: Architecture, music, environmental issues.

My style is achieved using acrylic paint and photocopy/ photographic collage. The result is often an impressionistic handling of architecture and interiors. My work can be more abstract depending on the subject matter. Due to the possibility of moving over the coming year, please contact (0325) 720747 for my location.

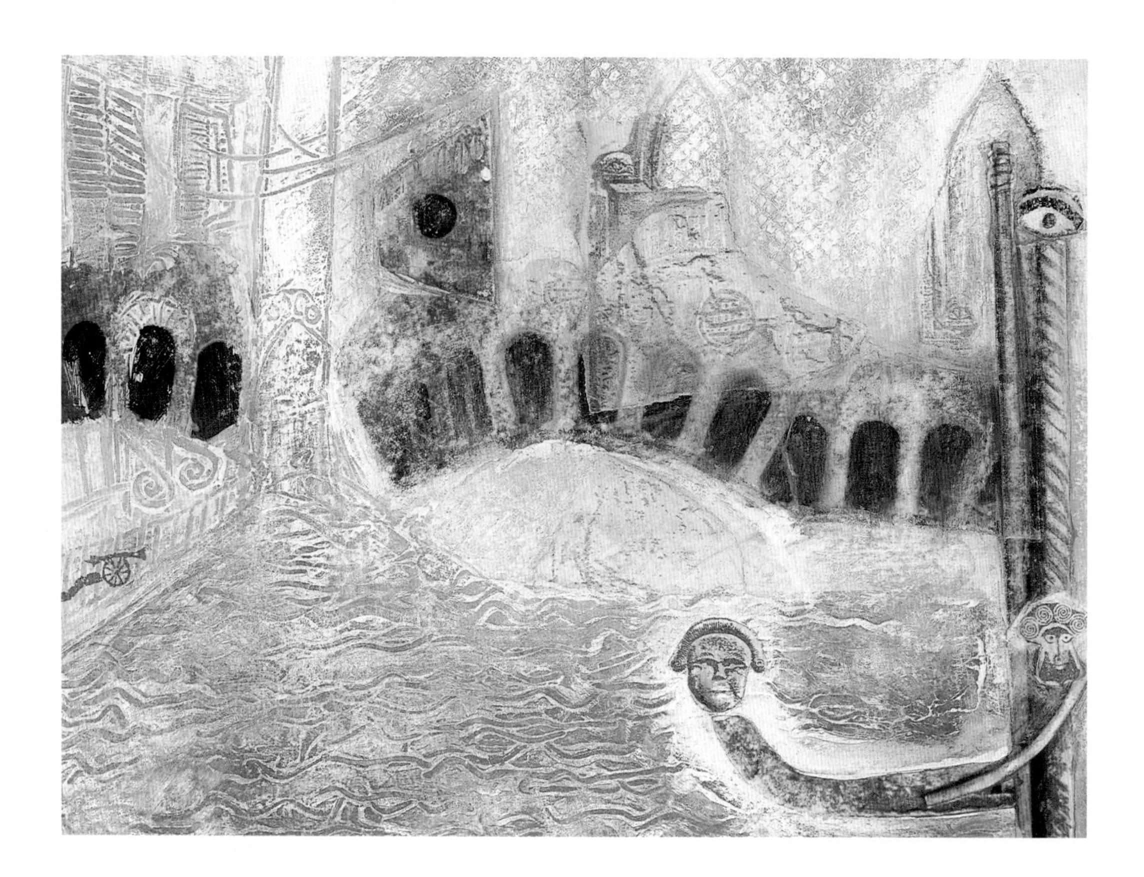

elsa houghton

22 Battlefield Lane
Wombourne
Staffordshire
WV5 0JL

t: 0902 892662

Title
"Alfonso on the Scrap-Heap Planet".

This story was developed and completed during my 2nd and 3rd year at college into a 24 page children's story book, as yet unpublished. The main character "Alfonso" can transform himself into a space rocket and submarine at very short notice. He travels into outer space where he meets all sorts of creatures, before being united with his soul-mate.

Title
"An Englishman Abroad"
The brief was a college project to illustrate a magazine article about British business-people venturing abroad.

nigel moore

14 Field Court Gardens
Quedgeley
Gloucester
GL2 6UD

t: 0452 722344

'La Vie Boheme' · An introduction of a poem by Fiona Pitt-Kethley, the well known poetess, authoress and female casanova.

georgios manoli

397 Whalebone Lane
North
Chadwell Heath
Romford
Essex
RM6 6RH

t: 081 597 2457
f: 081 597 2457

Unpublished Book Jacket for "The House of the Spirits" by Isabel Allende. Student project set by Stephen Kent (ex-art director "Penguin Books").

Johanna fernihough

26B Manchuria Road
Clapham
London
SW11 6AE

t: 071 585 2558

Graduate of Central Saint Martins School of Art and Design 1992. Since graduating I have been commissioned by Jonathan Cape and H.H.L. Publishing and won the "City University Business School" competition to illustrate their M.B.A. cover for 1993.

MBA Cover 1993 **1**

Tom Waits **2**
Book Cover

Autumn **3**

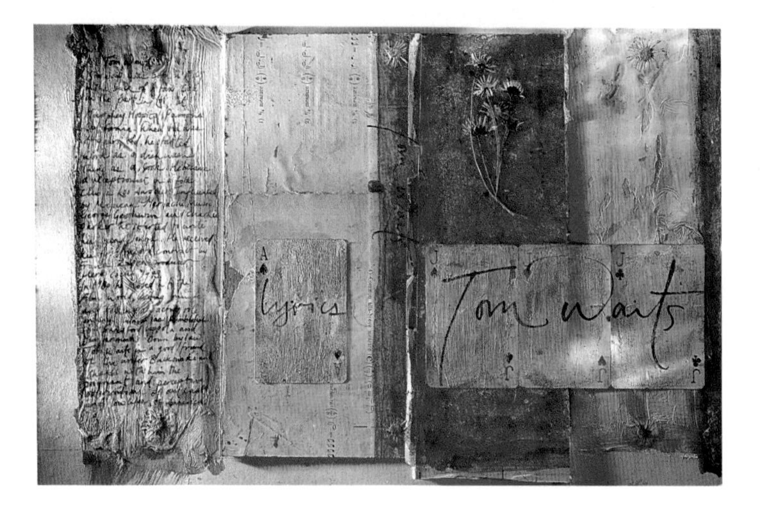

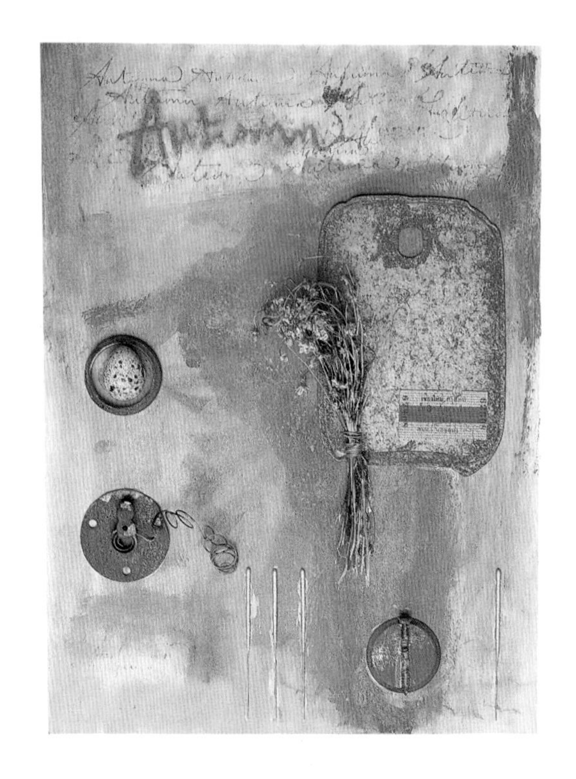

sue askey

c/o A.O.I.
29 Bedford Square
London
WC1B 3EG

(AOI)
t: 071 636 4100

martin johnson

52 Woodside Avenue
South Benfleet
Essex
SS7 4NY

t: 0268 753691

Title

Martian Johnson · simply a self-promotional contact poster, a fitting image I thought for the Newcomers section.

janet goddard

56 Trefoil Crescent
Broadfield
Crawley
West Sussex
RH11 9EZ

t: 0293 515089

I work predominantly in soft pastels with the inclusion of collage, and have recently begun to experiment with different media. Whenever possible I work from life as I find it not only more enjoyable but it provides me with better results. I will go on developing my skills as a freelance illustrator, in fashion related areas.

madeleine renee parker

11B Dagmar Road
Camberwell
London
SE5 8NZ
t: 071 701 1213

This is a City Lit Project, executed in bright inks, water colour, crayon and wax crayon. I have published with Norheimasund Books, Ferris Books, had work on television, and been in a number of exhibitions; the latest at St. Martin's in the Fields Crypt. I have drawn portraits and posters in shopping centres, church fetes, and a number of other venues. I also work in oils, pen/ink, black/white, and use pastels.

shaun swanton

2 Hillcrest Avenue
Chandler's Ford
Hampshire
SO5 2HS

t: 0703 270214

Shaun Swanton Illustrator · Graphic Designer. Completed HND at Portsmouth Art College.

Work produced for Airwave Gliders Limited Shalfleet I.O.W. These were logos for their new range of Voodoo Paragliders which took part in the European Championships. Posters for various Pizza Huts. Colour visuals for Animated Pixels Limited, Portsmouth. New commissions welcome.

DISABILITY DOES NOT MEAN LACK OF ABILITY

In 1794 this man lost the vision of his right eye. In 1797 his right arm was amputated, yet eight years later this man led the British Fleet to triumph in a devastating battle, that put an end to sea warfare for a century.

1991 and Great Britain has 6 million disabled citizens !

Only 31% of this figure are employed .

dti

pippa white

6 Lynwood Road
Tooting
London
SW17 8SA

t: 081 767 2754

Lust and Avarice - the seven deadly sins and their relationship with insanity. Two of a set of seven editorial illustrations in oil pastels. For a brief titled the Seven Deadly Sins (in a modern day context) which would supposedly be used for the Independent on Sunday Magazine discussing the relationship of sin and insanity.

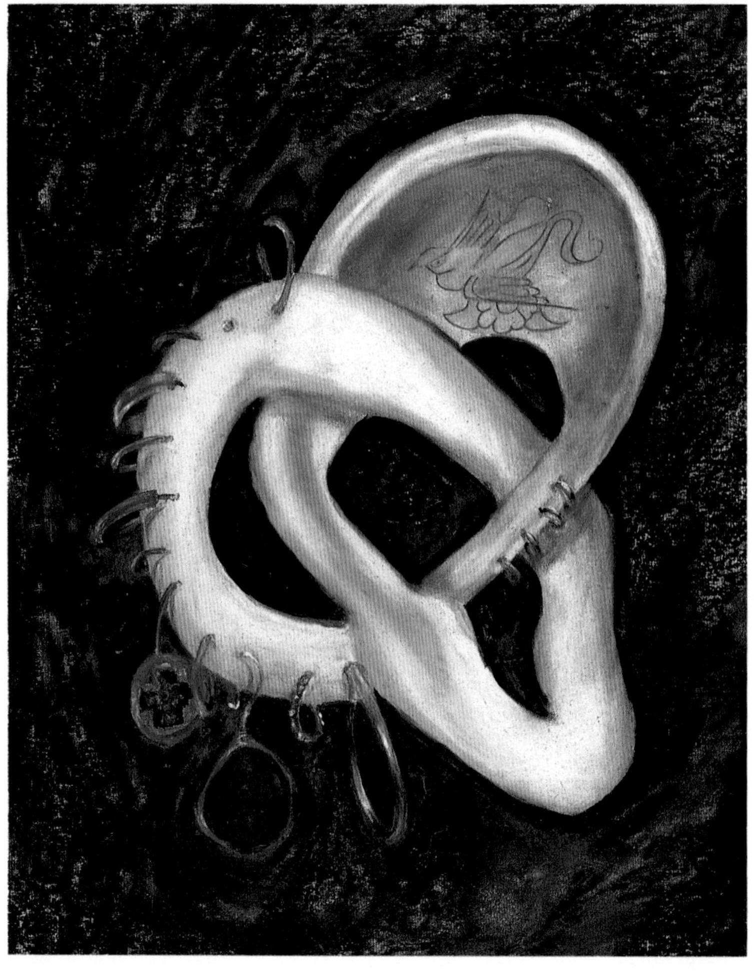

jessica rawlins

8 Pengelly Way
Threemilestone
Truro
Cornwall
TR3 6DP

t: 0872 40954

My distinctive style combines vibrant colours with stylised drawing and can be adapted to many subjects. I enjoy working in mixed media and my technique usually incorporates acrylic and pastel.

Clients include the Hahnemann Society for the Promotion of Health and Homoeopathy.

diane broadley

Bristol Craft and
Design Centre
6 Leonard Lane
Bristol
BS1 1EA

t: 0272 272878
f: 0272 297890

My work consists of an adaptable style in oil pastel, usually in colour but also some in black and white.

helen p c wright

4 Dobson Road
Langley Green
Crawley
West Sussex
RH11 7UH

t: 0293 535461

Mates
Friends for Life
Gouache
41cm x 51.5cm.

Images that beg a second look look whether speaking in a still, small voice or screaming loudly from the hoardings.

My objectives are diversity and individuality which I achieve using a wide range of mediums and techniques plus an abundance of zeal and enthusiasm.

Past clients include Abacus, The Independent on Sunday Magazine.

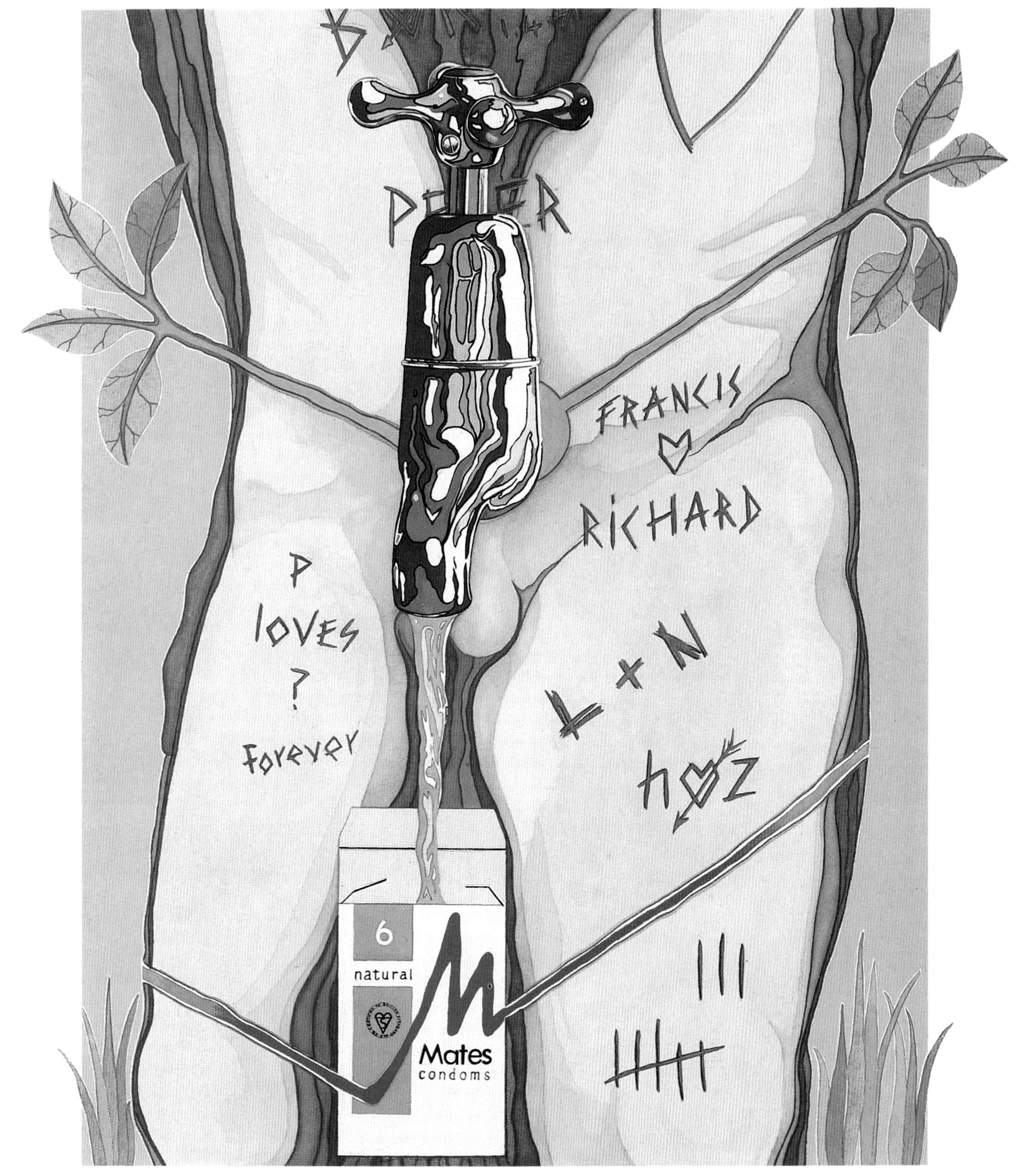

ailish moss

Studio 332
Stratford Workshops
Burford Road
Stratford
London
E15 2SP

t: 081 519 4512

Title
Aunt Spiker and Aunt Sponge.

Size
27.7cm x 22cm

Medium
Inks

One of six images for Roald Dahl's novel 'James and the Giant Peach'. "Aunt Spiker glared down at James as the magic beams slowly melted into the ground".

Ailish Moss is a graduate of Maidstone College of Art.

keith roberts

24 Ferndale Crescent
Kidderminster
Worcestershire
DY11 5LL

t: 0562 743298

After several years descending into a deep rut, I felt it was time to pursue a more rewarding way of life and so after quitting my job, I picked up my pencils and paints and embarked on a journey of discovery.

Firstly evoking the dormant creative interests of boyhood, which then slowly evolved into an insatiable appetite for all the visual arts, from abstract painting to TV soaps!

sarah adams

28 Clissold Crescent
Stoke Newington
London
N16 9BE

t: 071 254 2099

Studio
t: 071 278 2485

I specialise in lino-cut, colour and black/white. I also do figurative work.

Clients include
New Scientist, The Sunday Times, Reed Publishing, World Society for the Protection of Animals, Haymarket Publishing, Tax Journal. Also a recent winner of the Elle competition.

Illustration below commissioned by Reactions Magazine.

stuart harrison

184 Southgate Road
Islington
London
N1

t: 071 241 3230

Since the beginning of his career, Stuart Harrison has worked extensively in an editorial capacity for a large number of clients including Denis Publishing, MTV Hong Kong, EMAP Images, HHL Publishing, Passenger Clothes, IPC, Greater Manchester Passenger Exec, Longmans Educational Publishing and the BBC.

This piece is a self-generated brief entitled "Bangin' Hardcore". Future projects include a Franco-American animated film and a children's book, "The Silicon Pit".

simon roberts

29 Kingston Road
Southville
Bristol
BS23 1DS

t: 0272 661186
f: 0272 661186

Title
Around the clock

Medium
Airbrush gouache

Commissioned by
Sarah Sprosen

Agency
Sore Thumb

Client
Unisys

The artist was commissioned to design and illustrate the delivery of goods around the clock. One of a series of illustrations for the brochure.

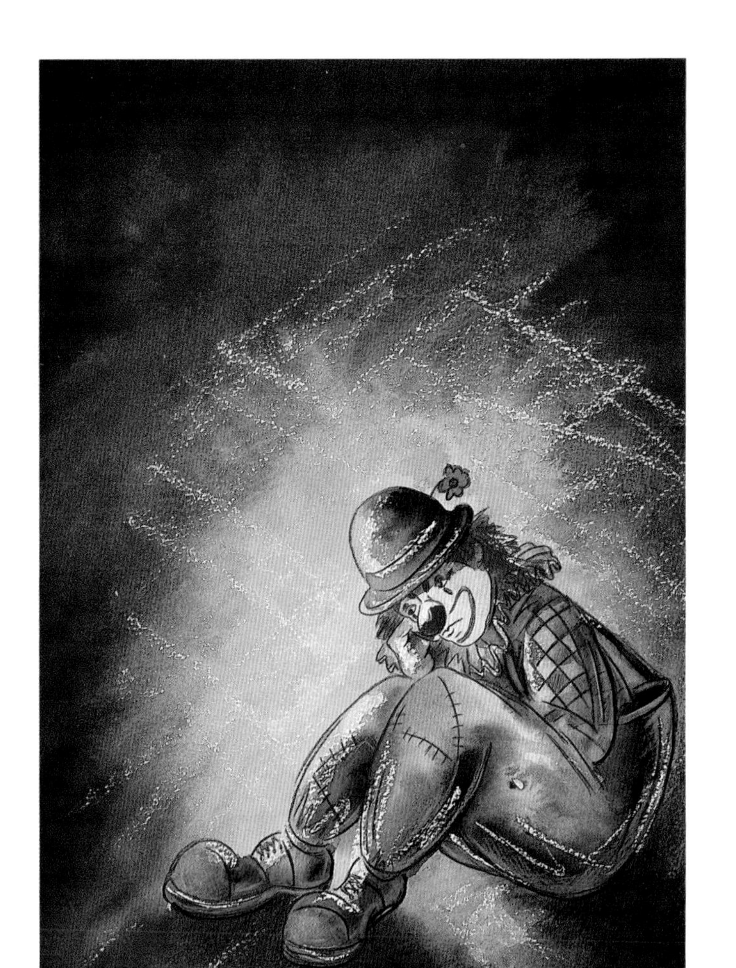

debbie tarbett

Gissons House
Kennford
Exeter
Devon
EX6 7UD

t: 0392 832289
f: 0392 833303

Self-promotional work using watercolour and colour pencil. To portray 'A sad face behind the clown's smiling make-up'. Also a more light hearted editorial illustration entitled 'Pie in the sky' concerning cuisine on Concorde.

2 Meadow Park
Cabus
Garstang
Nr Preston
PR3 1RE
t: 0995 606108

nicholas pain

mark hudson

20A Cloudesley Square
London
N1 0HN

t: 071 837 1911
f: 071 490 0063

fiona osbaldstone

195 Woodlands Road
Ditton
Aylesford
Kent
ME20 6HA

t: 0622 718377
f: 0233 712460